SECOND EDITION

Writing What You Know

How to Turn Personal Experiences into Publishable Fiction, Nonfiction, and Poetry

Meg Files

ALLWORTH PRESS
NEW YORK

23 22 21 19   5 4 3 2

Published by Allworth Press, an imprint of Skyhorse Publishing, Inc. 307 West 36th Street, 11th Floor, New York, NY 10018.

Allworth Press® is a registered trademark of Skyhorse Publishing, Inc.®, a Delaware corporation.

www.allworth.com

Cover design by Mary Belibasakis

Library of Congress Cataloging-in-Publication Data is available on file.

Print ISBN: 978-1-62153-511-9
Ebook ISBN: 978-1-62153-517-1

Printed in the United States of America

BOOKS BY MEG FILES

Meridian 144

Home Is the Hunter and Other Stories

Lasting: Poems on Aging (editor)

The Love Hunter and Other Poems

Galapagos Triptych: Three Ways of Seeing the Galapagos Islands (with Sally Cullen and Susan Reimer)

The Third Law of Motion

For
all my special students
all my special teachers
and, as always, for Jim

ACKNOWLEDGMENTS

Thanks to all my students who let me try out exercises on them and to those who allowed me to use their words. Thank you all, especially Gina Franco and Laura Van Etten, for forcing me to consider and articulate my advice, and for sometimes listening to it. Your devotion to your writing inspires me.

I am indebted to all the writers and teachers who have taken me seriously, especially Joanne Greenberg and Laurence Lieberman.

Deep thanks to my sisters and my father for their endless faith and support. I am grateful to Jim—who taught me more about writing than he knows—for his encouragement, advice, and endless source of stories.

CONTENTS

INTRODUCTION

When I was seven years old, I believed I was going to die. Not just someday, as even then I knew we all were. No, I wasn't even going to get to wear my new spring coat and black patent shoes.

In the hospital room, which my parents could visit only two specified hours a day, a mean nurse tried to make me swallow a pill the size of a Ping-Pong ball by holding my mouth shut until a doctor came in and let me spit the nasty pieces into his hand. Another nurse carried a tray to my bedside table, and on the tray was what looked like a small cage, covered with a white cloth. "I'm going to give you an animal," she said. That's when I got an early lesson in language. "Animal" and "enema" may *sound* alike, but they're different. Altogether different.

I'd been diagnosed with leukemia. Nobody said, "You, little girl, are going to die now, even before the coloring of the Easter eggs." But I knew. My mother brought me a giant stuffed Easter rabbit too early. Case confirmed.

There's a black-and-white photo of me propped against pillows with that tall, stiff rabbit beside me. I'm wearing a bed jacket. My hair has been brushed and arranged on my shoulders. I look as if I'm trying to be brave. Little girl's last photograph. It was the one that would be in the newspaper, no doubt.

My parents bought me a Dale Evans wristwatch so I'd know when visiting hours neared—and maybe to show me I wasn't dying, for it was too expensive to waste on someone who wasn't going to be around to appreciate it. See? Time would keep on going for me, right along with the pistol in Dale's hand, ticking off the seconds.

There in the high hospital bed, I wrote my first poems. They rhymed (badly). They were about wanting to fly and wondering why I couldn't.

Then I didn't die.

I left the hospital, dramatically, by wheelchair. I was home in time to eat the last of the hard-boiled eggs, with green and red and blue dye bleeding through the shell to the rubbery egg flesh. I had to wear brown lace-up corrective shoes, not the black patents. But I had not died.

I'd been misdiagnosed, really. Yet I understood the syllogism: I'd written poems and I hadn't died. Therefore, poetry saved my life.

Now I think of that flicking hand on the watch counting down the years. For me, writing and mortality are forever bound.

Maybe writing is still saving my life.

To be human is to want to figure things out. To be human is to hunt for meaning, to make sense of our seemingly random lives. And we have a powerful (and rather charming) way of giving shape and pattern to the chaos: We tell stories. We live fully by constructing and ordering scenes—that is, people doing things *for reasons*, whether known or unknown to themselves—and thus come to understand the random details and chaotic experiences of our lives.

Human creatures own the special ability to make sense in their minds. In the grocery store, I watch the couple in line ahead of me as they fuss and touch, and I see a kitchen with unpolished copper-bottomed pans and a table with three chairs, and, what?—a white cat. I move the man and woman around, making her put the milk in the cupboard by mistake and him place it in the refrigerator, and I understand the meaning of the extra chair. When the clerk asks, "Plastic okay?" I hope she doesn't see the sheen of tears caused by the little melodrama in my mind.

Humans own the special ability to make scenes in other people's minds:

> "At a village of La Mancha, whose name I do not wish to remember, there lived a little while ago one of those gentlemen who are wont to keep a lance in the rack, an old buckler, a lean horse, and a swift greyhound."

> *Can you believe it, right there in the backyard in the kids' treehouse—? So she told him . . .*

> "Frankie and Johnny were lovers, O lordy how they could love."

> *These two teenagers are parked out in the country, and the music on the radio is interrupted with a bulletin about an escapee with a hook instead of a hand . . .*

> "Here is Edward Bear, coming downstairs now, bump, bump, bump, on the back of his head, behind Christopher Robin. It is, as far as he knows, the only way of coming downstairs, but sometimes he feels that there really is

another way, if only he could stop bumping for a moment and think of it."

"Cain said to Abel his brother, 'Let us go out to the field.'"

See this hole? Your father fell asleep out in the car, waiting outside the hospital, and his pipe burned this hole in his Michigan State blanket, and that was the night you were born.

"He was an old man who fished alone in a skiff in the Gulf Stream and he had gone eighty-four days now without taking a fish."

We love stories in their various shapes—tall tales, great books, gossip, ballads, family history, and all—because their designs help us make sense of life not in the abstract but in the particular. Stories show events happening to a certain featured cast rather than to a generic humankind: Their universality rises out of their individuality. And this is the special appeal, the way stories engage us: They provide the entertainment of scenes. "The Joneses are getting a divorce for irreconcilable differences" won't do. We want the dirty details, the he-saids and the she-saids. We love stories for suspense: Events happen in a certain sequence—there's a story line, and things change. Even if we know the outcome in advance (no one asks, Oedipus did *what?*), even if we've heard the story over and over, there's the uncertainty of how and why and that little shiver of doubt—maybe you weren't born after all . . . or at least that night. We love stories because they happen to people. They may be real or made up; they may be stand-ins for people (Chicken Little, R2-D2); they may be ourselves. Events matter because we can live them along with other humans.

Stories share the characteristics of scene and details, of plot and suspense, of characters, whether they're factual, loosely based on true events, or invented. Stories can be shaped into poems, short stories, novels, personal essays, memoirs, hybrids, and crossovers.

We love stories because we *need* them. We live with great mystery swirling around us, pressing up against us, inhabiting us. From primeval slime to . . . me? From womb to tomb? What happened? What will happen? How? Oh, why?

Mythologies explain history, nature, religion, and the human psyche with stories—with scene (and Demeter made Persephone eat a pomegranate seed); with detail (Odin in his sky-blue hood); with plot (the quest for the Golden Fleece); with suspense (don't do it, Orpheus); and with character (Penelope with her loom). Now, today, as readers and as writers, we still need stories to explore the mystery. Stories have the power to say the unsayable.

This book will lead you to your stories, help vanquish the fears that may sometimes silence you, and lend the courage to explore both the known and the unknown. If you have a story you want to write, if you're struggling with a story, if you've written a story, this book will also give practical guidance in deciding whether to tell your stories as fiction, nonfiction, or poetry; in professional techniques; in listening to critics; and in revision. This book will show you how to shape your stories into incarnations of mystery and truth.

A woman at a writers' conference asked me, "What makes you think the world needs another book?"

We all know that what the world really needs is love, sweet love.

I happen to believe that stories and books can take us deeply into the world and its people, beauty and travail and horror and all, and if not to love, then to see and perhaps to change, to question, to experience, and to understand. And, yes, sometimes to love.

But I don't write for the world.

In his memoir *A Cloak of Light: Writing My Life*, author Wright Morris said that in a book he read as a young man he came upon the phrase "(f)etch me my cloak of light!" "Without any idea what the author meant, I knew I was the reader he had in mind. In the best of times, in the worst of times, the writer has within him his own cloak of light, and he travels with it wrapped around him."

The world may not need another story, another poem, another book.

But maybe you do.

1

TRUTHTELLING:
FINDING THE BEST STORY MATERIAL

Growing up shy, I wrote for two reasons. First was need, simple need, though I wouldn't have known to say so. Hiding in the basement rec room and tucked into a corner on the old brown studio couch, with one little light, I wrote my ponderings and poems in a diary that had a built-in lock. Now and then someone would drop dirty clothes down the laundry chute. They'd pick up two floors' worth of momentum and whump onto the linoleum beside the couch, causing me to lurch back into my perfectly normal and adequate life containing Buster the cocker spaniel, a grandfather with *Lady Chatterley's Lover* on his bookshelf (and it was my blessed job to dust his room every Saturday morning while he smoked cigars on the back step), and a little attic above the garage where my sisters and I raised mice. Then it was back to what I needed: my secrets set down in written words.

My public writing was for admiration. Every Saturday our mother took my sisters and me (fresh from the woods with Lady Chatterley, whew) to the Washington Square Public Library, where I worked my way from the YA section through the adult fiction alphabetically, from James Agee to Edith Wharton. My mother was an artist, and if I couldn't draw even a black cat on a moonless night, I could win her favor with clever poems and pretty descriptions. And the English teachers—from the dumpy old vice-principal's wife with crusty eyes to Mr. Smith, straight out of college, reciting "Annabel Lee"—I loved them all and their sometimes embarrassing passion for the written words of others. My essays were charming, my book reports (of course) passionate. I knew how to do it in college, too (my heart for an essay test). In creative writing classes, my sonnets and stories earned As and the admiring comments—"This is the most . . ." and "This is the best . . ."—from those I most admired.

Oh, but the private writing. There, in my childhood diary and college journal, were the secrets; and there, in the scraps of stories, were the hurts and doubts. Now I know the experiences and emotions were not unique, as they seemed, nor was I so alone as I felt. But I sensed then, and understand now, that this raw, messy, intense writing was the real stuff.

It wasn't that the public writing was dishonest. Rather, it was safe. (I recall a comment a teacher once wrote when I risked turning in a piece of my private writing: *Huh???*) The public writing was from the outside in, not the inside out. It was written with Mom and handsome Mr. Smith looking over my shoulder. It was coherent and smart and lovely. No one would ever write *Huh???* in its margin.

So I continued writing safe, made-up stories. One of my first stories in college was about a lonely middle-aged gay man hanging out at a gay bar. I wonder, now, why the professor of my writing class didn't say, "You know, Meg, you're a young college girl who doesn't know a single gay person. You've never been to a gay bar. And the only middle-aged man you know is your father. Why don't you try writing a story about a shy high school nerd?"

Then, still trying the public writing that would no doubt win me acclaim, I got an idea from *Life* magazine for a story about a white woman who'd grown up in Little Rock and, in 1957, had her picture in a magazine, with her fist raised and her face full of hate at the black teens integrating her school. Twenty years later, the picture is reprinted with an article called "Little Rock Revisited." My character must confront what she was and assess her change. It was a flop of a story, in spite of its potential, because I grew up in Michigan and never lived in the South. I didn't know the nuances of the South in the '50s, and I didn't know a thing about Southern guilt. (I knew plenty about Midwestern guilt, but it didn't seem to translate.)

I kept writing and writing, never seeing the disparity between what I needed—to explore my own most personal material—and what I wanted—publication, success, admiration. I wrote entire books. Rejected, rejected, rejected. What was I doing wrong? I tried to write good, clean prose. And I tried to figure out what would sell. The only answer was *nothing*, at least nothing I wrote.

Finally, I got mad. I wrote in my journal: *To hell with New York. I'm going to write the book I want to write and I'm going to make the prose as rich as I can, and I'm going to explore everything fully.*

I quit thinking about publication. I quit worrying about writing badly. I stopped thinking about what my family would think if I exposed our common history. I wrote the book I wanted to read. This time I wrote the book I *needed* to write.

It won't surprise you, of course, that this time I wrote a publishable book, one that has made even tough reviewers cry. I learned that readers didn't care about my formulaic stories when I myself hardly did.

Sparks fly with the fusion of want and need. It's a lesson I teach myself with each new writing, again and again.

What Are Our Stories?

Write what you know, writers are often instructed. Write what you want to explore, I add.

Beginning writers may wonder: Just what is it I know? Probably not much. So how the heck do I know what I *want* to know?

Experienced writers often understand that their best writing will come from their own pains and passions, yet may not know how to shape their own experiences into stories and essays and poems.

How do we find, explore, and transform our personal experience? How do we know what our real material is? Why should we write from personal experience, anyway, rather than invent? How do we expose family secrets and still stay in the will? How do we access buried material? How exactly is personal experience shaped into stories, essays, and poems?

If we could make a bargain here, it would be this: I will tell you the writing truths I know, and you'll dare to write your own truths. I'll buckle your seatbelt and send you driving into the storm. I'll make the lightning if you'll make the thunder.

On the second day of the creative writing workshop, we introduce ourselves and offer reasons for joining.

"I'm here to learn how to get ideas," Brad says. "I know how to write. I can write a bestseller, I know it, if I could just get a hot idea."

"Yeah, well," Joe jumps in, "I've already got this great idea. Based on that story in the paper—that guy who got buried alive? So in the first chapter, he gets involved with the Mafia . . ."

"I've already written ten chapters of this fantasy about magic and evil based on this game," Sophie says. "It's got zombies and elves and . . . I just don't know if I should self-publish or what."

I move us along. We'll have to talk later about the hazards of telling a story before and during the writing.

Shirley says, "I want to write, but I don't have anything to write about. My life has been so ordinary and boring. Born, raised, blah blah blah."

"That's not my problem," Marie says darkly. "I've got plenty to write about. I mean, plen-ty. But when I write about it, it comes out pathetic. Just lame."

Their stories will be wonderfully and wildly individual, I know, but their concerns are typical. You may share their questions, which are the big ones: What are our stories? How do we find them? Where do they come from? Who will read them? My hard lessons and the struggles of my students may help you recognize the sources of your own best material.

I began my novel *Meridian 144* with an idea. I'd always loved stranded-on-an-island survival stories, and I'd long had an interest (perverse, perhaps) in after-the-bomb stories. Yet none of the books ever quite satisfied me. Too often the stories fell into power struggles: newcomers versus natives, the tribe with the big guns versus the tribe with the big brains. Men were the protagonists. And they left things out. What if you don't know how to crack a coconut without a tool? What do you do when you run out of clean underwear? (Later a newspaper interview printed my grinning jacket photo and the headline: "What happens when the world's all gone and there's no pizza?")

So—knock hand on forehead—I got the hot idea of combining the two plot ideas. How about a book featuring a woman stranded on an island after a nuclear holocaust? (It isn't quite as bad as it sounds. I was living on a Micronesian island so I had my setting, and I did my homework on the likely effects of nuclear war.) The notion of telling the story I wanted to read was useful, yes. But I wrote—and trashed— five versions of chapter one. No matter how many notes I took about radioactive breadfruit, no matter how long I stared out my window at the flapping banana trees and the sea beyond, with its grades of blue, nothing was happening on the page.

Why?

Because, I finally figured out, stories aren't hot ideas.

Writers who believe they need a hot idea do very little actual writing, I've noticed.

Writers who come upon a hot idea and outline its plot in intricate detail end up with contrived paint-by-number stories, and when nobody wants to publish these shallow books, they turn angry and bitter. That's if they even complete the book. Usually, as with my student Brad, the enthusiasm for the hot idea cools enough after the seventeenth retelling that the writer simply drags the file named "Live Burial" to the trash basket. Command: Empty trash. Before it stinks worse.

Writers like Shirley, who believe they have no material because they haven't traveled down a piranha-infested Amazon river in a leaky dugout, haven't yet learned about their true and never-ending source.

Stories come from people. Not from ideas, not from plots. William Faulkner, in his 1950 Nobel Prize acceptance speech, gave us the key to our material: "the human heart in conflict with itself." I learned this in my own life, and years since, I know it is still the source of our stories.

After my mother died, I turned from my invented survival story first to silence, next to a journal, then to poems, and finally to short stories about bereft daughters. And when I understood that my novel's character wasn't an action figure to be manipulated through a prefabricated adventure but rather a flawed, complex, lost woman, I could write her story. When I understood that she was bereft in the world, and of the world, too, I began writing not a hot thriller but an exploration of the human urge toward destruction.

To Shirley, and to you readers who say nothing much has happened to you, I say: You grew up somewhere, somehow, with some sort of family. Oh, you have hundreds of stories.

Our direct experiences, the large tensions and small moments of our abnormal lives, are the unending source of our best stories. One of my favorite cartoons, by syndicated cartoonist Jennifer Berman, shows a huge room of seats with a banner announcing "Adult Children of Normal Parents Annual Convention." In the auditorium are two people.

At the same time, experience isn't merely what we have committed and what has been committed unto us. It is every action we might have taken, every word we didn't say. It is our roads untraveled. Experience is everything we've imagined. It is all we've observed, all we've read and heard and overheard and witnessed.

Grace Paley changed my writing life when I heard her say that she was able to revise her stories when she stopped thinking "good or bad" and started thinking "true or false." Now, when I write a first draft, as well as when I revise, I've stopped trying for lovely prose. Instead, I want merely to get down my character's or persona's truths. As you enter the world of your story, you too can ask: What is it like to be this person in this time and place, caught up in this web of trouble? What does this person notice? How does this person think?

Whether we're writing fiction or nonfiction, it is not facts we're after, not a recounting of actual events. It is essential truth we're hunting. And it is our own pains and passions that lead us to our true stories.

Truthtelling may dig into actual experience or sail into airier extrapolation and invention. Either way, it benefits our writing—and us—in many ways. One young writer gave this advice to his fellow students: Write all your essays in the nude. (Please, I hastened to add, not in the library or the coffeeshop.) He knew that baring ourselves, figuratively, lends an authenticity and emotional honesty to the writing; he knew that we are more likely to care about writings that emerge from our own material and that such concern is likely to entice readers.

One afternoon, a man seeking to join my fiction workshop asked, "What success rate do you have?"

"Success?" I asked. "Measured how?" I dreaded the answer: dropout rate, grades, publications.

"Reading interest," he said. "People want to read each other's stories."

That made my day. How do you answer that? "Ninety-five percent," I said.

Truth is partly in the shaping of the material. The raw data of experience are jumbled, contradictory, and random. Writing a story or an essay or a poem imposes a pattern of cause and effect, of connections to the mess of actual experience. Leonard Bernstein said that music is "cosmos in chaos." Stories give us, as all art does, order out of life's disorder. Even if the meaning is something out of an absurdist play—such as that there is no meaning—the story, with its people and grass and sky and conversation, by its tension and very form, has made meaning. Out of the chaotic mess of debris and darkness has been shaped an ordered universe or world or street corner.

How do you go about this shaping? Begin with your material. You can't so much choose it as recognize it. We'll talk later about story design. For now, begin with the willingness to dig into the territory that your life experiences have staked out for you.

Writing usually needs such solid ground beneath it. Truthtelling will make your places real. I couldn't pull off an Arkansas story, but I could plant a story in Southern Illinois because I spent enough intimate time there to know its details, dialects, and land. What landscapes do you know?

Long ago, my poetry teacher Laurence Lieberman said that not merely the experience but the texture of the experience must flow through the lines. Unless we know of what we speak, the only texture to our writing may be slick.

Looking inward leads you to your own most powerful writing. Beginning writers, like Brad in the creative writing workshop, who know the importance of originality, search the newspapers and the Internet and their imagination for what doesn't exist: a new story. The source of originality, though, is within—in your quirks, in your fascinations, in your obsessions. My fixation on the music of Gustav Mahler led me to write "The Pressure to Modulate," a story not really about Mahler but about a woman facing death. For years, I kept returning to an image of my husband making a perfect catch in left field until it led to "Serpentine." My captivation with coyotes led to "Coydogs," a story not about coyotes but about a young woman with some mother issues.

Private obsessions, small and large, are the door to originality and the key to unlocking it. Forget about what *seems* like good material or what experiences *should* have affected you or what your friends *say* you should write about. Instead, begin with the images and memories that won't leave you alone. Logic or reason isn't a factor, and you may have no notion of why certain pictures replay themselves in your head, though you'll almost certainly discover why as you write. Become like our late great family wolf, Cochise, who had a rawhide bone that he carried around, dropped and chewed on for a while, picked up and hid in our bed, and soon retrieved to carry around some more. What details and scraps of memory do you gnaw on and bury and unearth and gnaw on again?

Once you have your images, how do you know what your real material is? One easy answer is: whatever you don't want to write about, whatever you're afraid of. To that answer some writers, like Marie in the workshop, might say, "Heck, no fears here. My life is an open book. I've faced it. I've dealt with it." Others, like Shirley, will protest: "My conflicts are so petty. Who can get all worked up about something like the time I poured glue down my sister's throat?"

Merely thinking about your material may lead nowhere. Or everywhere! But with pencil on paper, or with fingers on keyboard, you may trick yourself into finding the material that will lead to strong and strange narratives.

At a writers' conference years ago, speculative fiction writer Harlan Ellison, emphasizing the need to unmask ourselves in the name of writing, asked, "What's the worst thing you've ever done?" Scanning the audience, he confessed to something naughty he himself had done and then told about a sweet young woman at another conference who said she'd never done anything bad, but then added, "Well, I did throw a lizard into a window fan once."

Ellison pointed to a woman in a middle row. "You. What's the worst thing you've ever done?"

"Oh, well, nothing," the woman said. "I haven't ever done anything really bad." Then abruptly she broke into tears and confessed that, five years earlier, she'd watched a man drown and done nothing. She'd never told her husband, who was sitting beside her at the conference.

"Was it because you couldn't do anything?" Ellison said. "Or you just didn't?"

"I don't know," she said. "I don't know."

I suspect Ellison may have received more than he needed, and the woman was upset enough to leave the conference. But the point was validated when she returned the final day with a strong and disturbing story.

Can you unearth your own strong or disturbing stories?

How Do We Know Our Stories?

Here are some equally nosy questions. You should answer them as honestly as you can and do it in writing, in the privacy of your own room. You should read your answers and then run them through the shredder. Why? Because here you're going to tell the naked, raw truth, and you don't want those pages discovered. The purpose is to mine your own best writing material, which is usually the most private, the most protected, the most secret.

For now, truth is raw. In the stories that grow out of it, it will be transformed, transmuted, told "slant," as Emily Dickinson advised. Once you've set it down, you may want to make a brief, innocuous list of potentially good material before you shred the gory details. Shredding is a good idea, not only to protect your innocent (or guilty) self, but because it will be easier to move from this surface of literal facts to deeper truths.

Your answers to the following probing questions will reveal your richest story material:

1. What has been the happiest moment in your life so far?

   A majority of adults of all ages, polled by Gallup, claimed it was—no, not their wedding, not the birth of a baby—but high school graduation. Depressing, huh?

   Your answer might lead you to a story such as Michel Faber's "Vanilla Bright Like Eminem," Roxane Gay's "North Country," or Susan Minot's *Evening*.

2. Describe a recurring dream. Or, if you can't remember one, describe a dream you haven't forgotten.

This is the subconscious at work, right? Fear and wish fulfillment and all that. Forget Freud. Forget Jung. What do you make of it?

Stephen King says his novel *Dreamcatcher*, as well as other stories, began in a dream.

3. Give yourself an alternate name. Choose an alternate occupation or area of study, unrelated to your present job or major.

An oncologist I know remade himself into a salmon fisherman. A family I know turned themselves into Aleta, Lance, and Septimus. Hooray for parallel lives.

4. Describe an incident that nobody but you seems to remember. Or write about an incident that others recall differently than you do.

If it's true that we remember the important things, if how we remember something reveals its significance, this question may lead you to a story such as Tracy Daugherty's "City Codes" or Robert Boswell's "A Walk in Winter."

5. What were your teenage years like?

Many successful writers, who were outcasts during their vulnerable times, turned to books to survive. Your answer might lead to a story such as Joanne Greenberg's "Merging Traffic" or ZZ Packer's "Drinking Coffee Elsewhere."

6. What are your five greatest fears?

Okay, I stole this from Stephen King. Except he asked for ten.

7. What was the most traumatic incident or time period in your adult life?

One writer confessed to herself something she'd done to her daughter. Then she realized it was the same as her answer to question five, except that it was what her mother had done to her. Out of this connection that she'd never before made came a very fine essay.

8. What's the worst thing you've ever done?

Guess you saw that one coming.

9. What should you probably delete from your search engine history?

(Hey, it was all in the name of writing research.)

10. What are your secret guilts? What do you hope nobody ever finds out? What's behind the mask?

Write it.

Now, shred your answers.

We'll be looking at how to use this raw material, how to shape it and transform it. Now, though, it's enough to have discovered some of your deepest material in its raw state. And having found it, you can, you *should,* dispose of the evidence. The discoveries will stay with you—I have no doubt.

The material you have revealed to yourself will give you dozens, even hundreds, of stories. But few readers, no matter how well they know you, will be able to match your answers with the writing they inspire.

Writers are sly, creating parallel lives not only to protect the guilty (including themselves) but also to reveal truths that are beyond the facts. Facts *are* stranger than stories. They belong to chaos. Even the weirdest writing gives us a patterned universe.

The source of writing is in our personal charged thunderclouds, dark or silvery. Climb onto Thor's chariot and take the ride. Our best narratives—our own true stories—are made of thunder and lightning.

In the beginning (and we're always beginning), many writers want balmy weather. They may believe readers seek sunny reassurances, but focusing on what they believe readers want is sometimes an excuse to avoid facing the fears that keep them from walking unprotected into the storms.

When she was my student, writer Laura Van Etten said she was "freaked out about writing." She knew she wanted to write, but "I had a big fear of saying something offensive." Afraid to write from her own experience, instead she invented. "I remember writing this very, very bad piece about a girl who's just received her satanic bible in the mail and her plans to do a ritual with an animal heart (that she was currently ordering)."

Out of the nosy personal questions exercise came a bold story about a girl sent away by her mother to a mental institution. "It was the first time I tackled personal material," Van Etten said, "and it was the most important story I ever wrote because it led me to believe that my experiences and my voice had value." She learned that "it's okay to write about this stuff. . . . Maybe I can make sense out of this stuff; maybe I can make something good out of this stuff, maybe I have actually found something I care about."

Here's a scene from Van Etten's story "Winter Sun":

They all sat in rows. One row down the side of each table. Windows lined the walls in this room, and the artificial bright yellow lights seemed sickly in contrast to the brown and dim of the real world outside. A nurse stood by each table. A guard. Watching. Each movement of food to mouth. Each squeeze of ketchup. Jamie pushed the gray burger to the side of the tray and tried to focus on the apple instead. She smelled perfume hovering over her and turned to the scented nurse.

"No more than one cut per piece of food, Jamie."

"What?"

"We are trying to break compulsive food patterns. Obsessively cutting food into little pieces is one of them."

Jamie looked around at the others, but they all looked down quickly. "What are you talking about? It's an apple. I cut it, twice, sections, quarters, ya know, to eat?"

"I know this may seem like a small thing, Jamie, but it's one of the rules. You can go ahead and eat the apple this time, it's just a warning."

"A warning? I am getting a warning for cutting an apple in two? Yeah, what a rebel, good thing you caught this one early on." Jamie took the knife and hit the apple again. A piece flew off the tray. "Oh my god, it's out of control, confiscate the apple, call for backup."

Another nurse walked over. "Jamie, you have made it perfectly clear how you feel about the rules. Eating is a difficult time here, and controlling this environment is for your sake. That is why there are rules. All you are accomplishing by this display is the disruption of the other girls' meals. Do you understand that?"

"I understand I'm being disciplined by the food patrol for eating an apple incorrectly. Maybe there's a manual—I don't know anything about oranges, you know." Jamie shoved her tray away and refused to break the stare of the nurse.

"Okay, Jamie. We're going to take your dinner tray into your room and you'll have to eat your evening meal in there. I'm sorry." She leaned over Jamie and lifted the tray. Shelly was staring at her, there was a dumb kind of awe. Cows too stupid to move unless an electric prod hit 'em in the ass. Jamie finally stood and followed the nurse down the hall.

The nurse set the tray on the end table, pulled up a chair for Jamie, and sat on the bed. Jamie stared at the hacked apple, the bare burger. Finally the nurse spoke. "Jamie, we don't like to do this, but it's a matter of protecting the others."

"Oh—of what?" It was unexpected and Jamie felt the shift of things just outside her grasp, like something sliding inside her. "Protecting people from me?" Her eyes were hot and burned before she could look away. She bit hard into her lip. She felt the wet on the lower lid and knew if she blinked, the tear would fall. She swiped at her eye and hit it harder than she meant. *Fuck you. Give me some kind of guilt trip. I didn't put them in here. I didn't agree to your rules. Your plan to make life easier for a bunch of fucked-up kids.*

"I know this is hard for you, Jamie. You need to finish your tray, though."

"You don't know what's hard. Can you—just please, am I allowed to be alone at all? Listen, I don't care about the food, can I just be alone? Please."

"Once you've finished the meal, Jamie, then I can leave."

Jesus. Jamie grabbed the burger in her fingers. She ripped it in half and shoved it in her mouth. She swallowed whole chunks of cold, stiff meat. She gulped the milk and stuffed the apple sections in her mouth. Slowly then, she traced her index finger carefully around the edge of the tray. She raised her eyes to the nurse's and brought her finger up to her lips and sucked it noisily. "All gone."

The nurse stood up. "I'm sorry this was so hard for you, Jamie." When she left, Jamie moved to the edge of the bed. It was still warm from where the nurse sat. She stared out, into the night and the black of the courtyard. Her stomach hurt.

My workshops practice a rule—don't ask, don't tell—that has nothing to do with gays in the military and everything to do with the use of personal material in writing. The controversial policy of DADT has been repealed, but don't-ask-don't-tell still holds for the writing workshop. No one is allowed to ask another writer in the group, "Did that really happen?" No writer is allowed to defend an event in the story by insisting, "Yes, but it really did happen just that way!" No writer is allowed, as interesting as the comments might be, to explain the personal origins of what finally is on the page, even if the work is an essay or memoir.

The rule keeps a clear separation between the writer and the writing and allows the objectivity necessary for discussion and revision. More importantly, it makes the workshop a safe place to take the risk of exploring personal material.

So I never knew what in Van Etten's answers to the nosy personal questions led to "Winter Sun." I only know that the exercise excavated strong material and gave her the courage to explore it and transform it into story. The scene's power comes from its vivid detail, certainly, but mostly, I think, from its willingness to get intensely close to the character Jamie and her pain.

This might be a true story:

A friend having tea with Thomas Hardy's wife asked, "Did Mr. Hardy have a good day of writing?"

"Oh, I'm sure of it," Mrs. Hardy answered. "I could hear him sobbing all afternoon."

What's a good day or night of writing for you? Perhaps it's when you've used your little silver key and opened the book of secrets and lost yourself as you shaped them into a story, an essay, or a poem. Lost yourself and found yourself. Perhaps it's later when, back in the tangible world around you, you are quietly full and satisfied because you know you have written something true.

Sobbing is allowed.

2

FACING DOWN THE MONSTERS:
QUIETING THE FEARS THAT HOLD BACK STORIES

"I leaped headlong into the Sea," wrote Keats on the experience of writing his long poem "Endymion," "and thereby have become better acquainted with the Soundings, the quicksands, & the rocks, than if I had stayed upon the green shore, and piped a silly pipe, and took tea & comfortable advice."

For writers, that green shore is a pretty place, a sweet place to hang out. We know its gentle flora and fauna, its bobwhite and dragonflies, its buttercups and soft grass. It is a safe place. The worst that can happen there is an ant or two in the potato salad.

Those who rest on the shore may write some lovely poems, some clever tales, some suitable-for-the-grandchildren recollections. However, it is only by jumping into the deep that we may (sometimes) create fresh, surprising, or profound writing. We may pass seaweed strangely blossoming underwater on our way down; we may encounter an ill-tempered anaconda powerful enough to crush a deer; we may discover odd creations such as the dugong with its front limbs like arms and, at the other end, not legs but a tail. We will find strange beauty, danger, and bizarre connections.

In the depths we may find squid making ink clouds around themselves or white eyeless fish, for some memories want to hide and some images want to be blind.

It is only by jumping into the murky and the unknown that we stand a chance of discovering our truths.

Stop and Write

(And do write, not think. Trust me here.)

1. What material—experiences, people, stories, whatever—do you want to write about but haven't?

2. What are you writing or have you written that is stuck or stalled?

3. What stories, essays, or poems have you begun but given up on, abandoned, left unfinished?

You want to write? So what's the problem? Just write.

If only it were so easy.

Other things we want to do—and love to do—are easy. Take a hike? All right! Put on your boots, leash up the dog (bandana optional), and head up the trail. Make a sweet evening? Buy candles, check Netflix, order pizza. No sweat.

Write? Sharpen those pencils, fire up that computer, and onward!

If only it were so easy.

Writing is play or should be much of the time, but it's different from the other pleasures of our lives. For one thing, it's solitary. Whether we finally show the writing to a writers' group or an editor, the *act* is solitary. Other activities we may love, such as reading, running, or watching movies, can also be solitary, but they don't require the private, almost secret separation from others. Even if your favorite spot is a coffeehouse, writing is an exclusionary activity.

My student Janice signed up for my fiction workshop semester after semester. She didn't need the credit or, after a couple rounds, the lectures, but she had a jealous family resentful of her "self-indulgent" time away from them while she wrote. As long as she was taking a class, her writing was her homework (emphasis on *work*), and that was okay with them.

I know a group of professional writers who meet regularly to write together. They do not talk. They are in a room together doing their solitary writing. I can't imagine it for myself, exposing my compulsive pencil-sharpening and who knows what other tics, but for them this is the solitude within the community.

Even reading isn't exactly solitary but a *pas de deux*—the reader and the author dancing together, though in ways neither partner fully knows. Writing—that's something else: That's you dancing with yourself.

So much seems to be at stake with writing. There are those who take their games seriously, for sure, but for many, writing equals identity. Such writers don't need a jealous family to give them a hard time. They can manage to scold and accuse quite nicely on their own, thank you.

Because of its nature, writing comes packaged with frustrations, fears, and inhibitions. Batteries included.

Monsters

My novel *Meridian 144* is the story of Kitty Manning's survival on a South Pacific island after a nuclear holocaust. It's not, I hope, merely an adventure story (though one reviewer did call it a "fast-paced gender thriller," whatever that is). It's the story of Kitty's life before she retreats to the island, of her relationships with her mother and her husband. Most of all, it's an exploration of Kitty's destructive nature and of our species' apparent obsession with destruction.

To tell these stories, I had to deal with two monster fears. The first was the fear of my family. It was comparatively easy to say to hell with publishers; my family posed more problems. A shocked aunt had already burned her copy of a magazine containing a story of mine. (Well, all right. The magazine was *Playgirl*. It was my first national publication. My proud father went to the newsstand and bought two dozen copies. He sent them to all the relatives. Truth is, I doubt if the shocked aunt actually read the story but just opened the magazine to find photos of guys in loincloths wielding machetes, which always looked dangerous to me, and her niece's story surrounded by ads for strange, um, products.)

What would happen if I wrote about my childhood pains and my sometimes ambivalent feelings about my mother, if I reshaped family history? What would my sisters and my father think? If Kitty, having caught her mother's neediness, looks for something like love in adulterous affairs, would my husband start feeling his brow for the cuckold's horns?

I tried to banish this monster with Faulkner's magic words: "If a writer has to rob his mother, he will not hesitate; the 'Ode on a Grecian Urn' is worth any number of old ladies." *Oh right*, the monster growled. *Your mother is dead. The family is grieving. And now you're going to rob her?*

That fear's monstrous big sister was my fear of self-exposure. I was afraid of exploring my pains, fears, and guilts. I was afraid to probe my secret heart. What would I learn about me if I exposed it, bloody and pulsating, on the page?

I'll explain how I dealt with my monsters. But first, let's look at yours.

Writers, and all humans, have a multitude of complicated and unknown-to-them ways of protecting themselves. The mind is a clever thing, and one of its goals may well be to help its particular human survive. Most of us, from time to time, should be grateful for such care. But these self-protecting strategies can actually hinder our stories. When the poem you're struggling with feels superficial, when the short story you're trying to write is stalled, when your memoir-in-progress just isn't working, consider that you may be protecting yourself with layers of clothes and a parka on top when what the writing needs is the bare, naked truth.

A hopeful writer in one of my workshops confessed, "I have to admit, I'm not about to bare my soul in public any more than I would walk naked into the street. Neither would be a pretty sight."

Some writers will stay on the shore fully clothed, slathered with SPF 30 sunscreen, beneath an umbrella. I invite you, though, to strip down at least to your bathing suit, if not to your birthday suit, and to jump into the sea.

How do you do this? First, try identifying the inhibitions and fears that may keep your writing too safe.

Stop and Write

(Once again, I say let your fingers do the walking rather than letting your brain do the talking.)

1. What holds you back from the stories you want to write (or know you need to write) but haven't written?
2. What stories have stalled on you? What stories have you left unfinished or abandoned?

Name Those Monsters

Identifying the fears that inhibit your honest writing is the first step to subduing them. Perhaps some of these monsters are on your list.

The Inner Mom

Workshop student Shirley, who used to fear she had no material worth writing about, now fears "hurting family members by revealing painful family history."

What will her family think if she writes the truth? Will they be hurt? Angry? What will they think of her? Will she be disowned, excommunicated, banished?

"My mother's voice is always in my head," she said.

"Mine, too," another writer in the group added. "And my mother's dead."

Bare Naked Cannibals

Fear of others' reactions extends beyond family. Shirley put it into words: "I always worry what other people will think, especially those who are important to me and whose opinion of me is something I value. If I feel the writing will reflect negatively on me, that feels threatening. If it might reflect negatively on them, that's even scarier."

What will friends, coworkers, even anonymous readers think of you if you expose yourself? Or worse, if you expose them? If you put them on a platter and serve them up? Will they be offended, shocked, hurt? Will you lose their friendship or respect?

Born Too Loose

. . . Or too uptight or cold-hearted or stubborn or volatile or impatient or stupid or prideful or downright wicked. What if you discover, in the depths of the sea, that your worst fears about yourself are true?

Joe, my student who was ready to abandon the notion that stories come from hot plot ideas, nevertheless had a hard time with my nosy personal questions. At question number four on my list, I heard him mutter, "Oh, let's not go there."

Roadkill

Some writers, willing to jump into the sea, may have a clear notion of what they're going to encounter on the way down. But therein lie additional concerns.

"My own experiences will be too boring to readers," one says.

"Mine will be too depressing," says another.

Many resist bringing back to life experiences safely in the past, flattened by time and memory. One writer acknowledged that he didn't want to "revisit painful memories so that they became alive again—all the sorrow, shame, unfinished business, things left unsaid, things said for which I have deep regrets."

Another wanted to write about a rape but was held back by "the power of putting words to paper; the necessity of going very deeply into the experience, remembering how I felt, noting the details—the room, the rapist, the aftermath."

A related inhibition can be seen in another student writer, Marie. She fears that she will end up trivializing her own life by not getting it right in her stories. "I worry that I don't have the craft to do it, that it would turn out badly and the material would be wasted. At times

I've tried writing autobiographically, but I wasn't able to transform the material into art. The whole process left me feeling kind of sick."

Point Blank

On the blank page or screen, all things are possible. The perfect writing, in which each word and punctuation mark capture the profundity of the real experience, the power of the emotion, and the ideal poem or story in the mind—this perfect writing lies beneath the page. The blank page hides the invisible, but it is still there, under the silence.

No wonder the blank page frightens writers. Once they mark it up and mess it up with actual words, the illusion disappears.

The blank page is also the unknown, that murky water. If even a toe is dipped in, piranhas may be waiting for just such a morsel. Or, equally scary, maybe nothing at all awaits.

In *Ghost Girl*, Torey Hayden describes a child who suffers from elective mutism, a little girl who for psychological reasons refuses to speak.

For you, what keeps the blank page blank? What silences you?

Fear of Not Flying

What if you write something that goes nowhere? What if the writing is bad, by anyone's measure? What if your most trusted readers don't get it? What if it never gets published? What if you loft your writing and it plummets straight to the cold ground?

Fear of failure inhibits many, but I've known some who are equally inhibited by success. A writer who struggled for years with appreciation from only his writers' group finally won a prestigious fiction award. Good! I thought. Now he's on his way. What we've been telling him all along has been validated.

Instead, it shut him down. He confessed, "I'm afraid I'll never be able to do it again."

Success makes demands: Get serious, don't drop the ball, live up to your promise. Many are ready to quit while they're ahead.

Stop and Write

(You know the drill: Take pencil in hand.)

1. Are there stories you were afraid to write but wrote anyway?
2. If so, what concerned you about writing those stories?

3. How did you overcome your fears (or try to, anyway)?

4. How do you feel about the resulting stories?

5. What advice can you give yourself to quiet your monsters?

After answering these questions, one writer added: "Here's something interesting. In writing this down, I find I can actually answer some of my own questions. Maybe I just need to continue writing about what's holding me back and then get on with it."

Identifying the fears that inhibit your honest writing was the first step to quieting them. Developing strategies to tame and subdue them is the second step. Perhaps my own lessons of how I dealt with my monsters will give you ideas.

Facing Down My Monsters

I subdued, if not banished, my own monsters by examining my purpose in writing. Back when I was trying to psych out the market, I wrote stories that would help readers do what I believed they wanted—to escape. The result was formulaic—action plots carried out by characters pulled from central casting.

With *Meridian 144*, at last I wrote to explore. The book allowed me to work out my own torments, to write down my fears, and to work through them. For some time I'd been in despair about the state of the world. We seemed bent on doing ourselves in, if not through nuclear war, then through pollution and general disregard for the planet. Writing the book allowed me to explore this destructive tendency and to see the fear that is at its heart. And while I might never accept the fear, I achieved a certain relief in acknowledging it.

This fear of our general destruction, while real, was also only abstract. My grief over my own mother's death was real and specific, as only our personal griefs can be. When she died, I simply could not accept that she was gone from the world. I cried again when I wrote about the death of my character Kitty's mother. (It's that funeral scene that has made reviewers cry, too.) By writing my mother's story, or parts of it, I know her as I never did before. Rather than following Faulkner's maxim and robbing her, I honored her with understanding. By writing that Kitty's mother was absolutely gone from the world, I put my mother back in mine and made sense of her mortality—not by offering easy answers or sentimentalizing, but by shaping, by making what I'm egotistical enough to call art.

Perhaps the fears brought up by my monsters kept my intentions pure—to write not to expose or sensationalize or justify myself or exact revenge, but to look through the facts of my life and of the world for truth. As I wrote, I took the facts of my experience, sifted through memory, and selected, altered, and invented, working the raw material into the shape of essential truth.

Robert Frost used to speak of poems as occupational therapy, something like the ashtrays and wallets that people in institutions make—something to give order to lives in chaos. My Pennsylvania Dutch grandmother used to cover big jugs and birdbaths with putty, into which she pressed buttons, bits of glass, medals, bottle caps, and all sorts of trinkets. She'd take all these random odds and ends, without any apparent connection to each other, and make a shape out of them. That's how I think of my books, too. They're full of real and imagined fragments, scraps, bits and pieces, which are put into patterns that make sense of the chaos of the real world, and of memory, too.

When my monsters growled and snapped, I reminded myself that nobody was forcing me to write. When I thought of all the rejections and grumbled that after all my effort and suffering, New York owed me, I reminded myself what writer Joanne Greenberg once said: "Just because I want to do it, there's no rule that says the world owes me a living." We make our own rewards. I spent four years writing *Meridian 144*, telling myself the story I wanted to read and looking at my past, my guilts, my passions. On the morning after I'd stayed up late sending Kitty to her mother's funeral, a friend noted my bright eyes and asked, "What do you know that the rest of us don't?"

Despite my fear, my family did not cast me out. My sisters found reading the book sometimes painful. But we talked more, and more honestly, after that. My husband, who knows the ways of writing, admitted to a bit of uncertainty, but he didn't give my side of the bed to the dog. And my father was nothing but proud. He lurked in the retirement community library, accosting anyone wandering near the fiction shelves. "Looking for something good to read?" he'd ask. In truth, the only unchanged relationship was with my dog, who was in the book but never read it. (Dead at age sixteen, the great-hearted Cimarron never had the chance to play herself in the movie. I suppose she'd have needed a stunt double anyway.)

Every time I settle into the world of a new book, I try to remember that our own pains, fears, guilts, and passions are the raw material from which we shape our best writing. Those who read our work and want to know how "true" it is will never know the real answer. It doesn't matter whether we deny all or explain the ways that writers distinguish between *facts* and *truth* or even tell them, "Yes, it all happened just this way."

So what? I ask myself. Staring down monsters changes us all and keeps us vital. I remember that writing's purpose is not to provide escape from life; it is to explore life. Why should we waste our time and talent and white paper on lies?

Facing Down Your Monsters

That hopeful writer who couldn't bear to bare himself because it wouldn't be a pretty sight was thinking of the beholder's eye. When he writes, there's a judgmental reader looking over his shoulder, pointing out flab and hairy warts.

He'll never create the stories he's capable of until he teaches himself to write with no beholder, no editor, no audience.

And he'll never create the stories he is capable of until he understands that they may not always *be* pretty sights.

When I asked my workshop students to describe their opinions of those stories they'd written in spite of their fears, they owned up to pride and gratitude. "I like the stories," wrote one. "They touch me and they challenge me into experiencing moments in a way I hadn't when they occurred."

And another: "They're the ones I get the most positive reaction on— that seem the most effective and the ones I'm most proud of. For a long time I only wrote stories that took place somewhere I loved being—the desert, in motels. When I started writing stories that scared me, that took me places I didn't like going, I felt it inhibited my writing. But the stories, once I got them out, were more powerful, deeper, and resonated more and were more widely praised in classes."

A facile writer who kept writing stories with clever plot twists and characters so flat they wouldn't bulge a George Foreman grill finally had a breakthrough and wrote a story featuring a complex character in a world of trouble. What happened here? I asked him. "You told me you were looking for a story from a limited point of view, in the voice of the character, a story of substance and significance to me. So that's what I did."

Sometimes we just need an assignment.

So here's yours.

Talk Back

How can we write "true" stories and still stay married, remain on the beneficiaries' list?

- Write the story as fully as you can. Tell all. Reassure yourself that you can always go back later and delete the nasty parts. Don't worry about who might eventually read it while it's still in progress.

  This mind-set got me through an entire novel I wasn't sure I could write for fear of family. Including scenes and details I thought I'd omit later led to the complex characters and the surprising connections that I am certain would not have surfaced on the page if I had skimmed over the offensive or disturbing parts, if I had remained *on* the surface.

  Later I found that nearly everything could stay, that it wasn't as bad as it seemed when I set the words down. I removed only one line that I knew would be hurtful.

  Whether or not you delete lines or entire scenes later on, write the first and second drafts *as if* you will.

- Change the names to protect the guilty.

- Don't show every family member everything you write. My first published story, a dreadful thing about twins in which one sister literally devours the other, appeared in a tiny magazine, circulation about twenty-five, and my sisters, who are twins, never read it. I hope nobody else did, either.

  Shirley, my student who was held back by her mother's voice in her head, said she overcame her fears this way: "Did it anyhow and damn the consequences. Plus, I never showed my mother my writing."

- Face the family. Talk about the ways writers use their material, altering and shaping. You're not justifying or defending or asking forgiveness, merely explaining. And you can use the writing to communicate. If your husband says, "Do you really feel the way this woman Willetta in your story feels about Edwin's habit of sucking on toothpicks until they're swollen, splintered, icky pulp"? then you can say, "Um, no, dear, I just made that up." Or you can say, "Well, sometimes it kind of gets to me, especially when you, I mean Edwin, leaves them piled up in a little logjam beside the remote."

Toothpicks are trivial, but whatever the material, a relationship might grow with honesty.

A writer in the workshop with Shirley, the one who never showed her writing to her mother, said, "The only way I could overcome the fear was to show the finished story to my mother. I paced around the kitchen furiously unloading the dishwasher while she read it. And afterward, she said she thought it was a good story."

We often fear a reaction more intense than what we get. I don't know a single writer sent by the family into permanent exile.

Eat Up

How can we write "true" stories and hang onto the friendships and good regard we so richly deserve?

- Extend the above "Talk Back" suggestions to friends.

- Get used to cannibalism. Those peopling the worlds we create on paper are often composites of folks we know. A coworker might serve as the prototype for the boss whom Willetta finally attacks with a staple gun after being driven mad by her husband's toothpick-sucking.

  (Note: It's a sort of grim fun to use writing to get even with enemies, but the satisfaction is short-lived. This brand of cannibal stew fails to nourish at the least, and contains salmonella at its worst.)

- Believe me when I tell you that people usually don't recognize themselves in our writing. My story "Repatriation of Remains" includes a rather mean portrait based on an acquaintance who, to my horror, showed up unexpectedly at a bookstore reading. Without a Plan B story on hand, I had no choice but to go ahead. Over my pages, as I read, I watched her laughing with the rest of the audience, and afterward she kissed me on both cheeks and carried on about my story's wonderfulness.

  Perhaps I'd disguised her sufficiently. More likely, she's like most humans who, inside themselves, don't recognize the view seen from the outside.

- Waste no time worrying about shocking or offending anonymous editors and readers. In fact, toning down, sanitizing, or prettifying the material, making it socially acceptable for polite company, is a good way to ensure that it won't ever have anonymous readers.

- Secrets aren't unique. Write your secrets. Readers will wonder, how did you know?

Bring on the Judge

How can we write "true" stories without exposing ourselves to ourselves?

- We can't. If it's true that the photographer is somehow present in every photograph, if it's true that every painting is somehow the artist's self-portrait, it's also true that writers inevitably reveal themselves in their writing. We're there in the details, the language, the voice, veiled in the shadows or bright on the illuminated page. We might try to run, but we can't hide.

- If we write not to defend our questionable actions or to argue for our virtues, but instead to explore our deepest material, we will surely emerge with greater understanding than if we'd stayed safely on that green shore. What if, in the writing, you confirm your worst fears about yourself? Okay, you'll feel bad. But you'll have new insights about who you are and why. Then you can use the knowledge to change.

  Usually, though, it's a matter of case *un*confirmed. It's worth taking the risk to come to know the truth: not prideful but pleasingly humble, not greedy but generous, not cold-hearted at all but compassionate and passionate. Oh, not guilty after all.

Raise the Dead

How can we tell our "true" stories without depressing our readers or ourselves?

- It's been said that all subjects but sex are inherently boring. In my long reading life, I've found that all subjects (yeah, including sex) are fascinating if the writer gives me the lowdown, the dirt, the skinny in all its behind-the-scenes, intimate detail. The stories that most engage us take us where we haven't been (on a riverboat full of vampires or into battle or behind a grocery store checkout counter) or take us more deeply into where we have lived (with fate, in foolish love, near nasty neighbors), and make us care about those who inhabit these strange and known worlds.

- A student of mine on a military base in Japan told me, "In my work I have to make serious decisions that affect people's lives. Life and death, sometimes. I read only for escape. I can't read or write all this depressing stuff you're asking." The course was a requirement, and so he had no choice but to read Dylan Thomas's poem "Do Not Go Gentle Into That Good Night" and Wilfred Owen's poem "Dulce et Decorum Est" and Katherine Anne Porter's "The Jilting of Granny Weatherall" and George Orwell's "A Hanging" and much more. As the term progressed, his writing moved from smart-aleck flip to thoughtful, and at the end he thanked me. Before the heavy stuff, he said, his work decisions might have been rational but often were easy or superficial as he ignored the humanity of those affected. He'd learned some things about wasted lives and fully lived lives, what "sweet and fitting" means in war, how to face death and how to face love, that the best decisions were informed by human understanding.

    Well, wow. Thank the power of writers' truths.

    Writing can uplift us and give us joy and triumph, but these are the intense releases after grief and pain, the culmination of writing that has first taken us to the depths.

- Certainly there are risks when it comes to raising the dead. Bad experiences are usually sealed into protective capsules or buried the requisite six feet under. Exposed to air again, they will no doubt stink.

    Reliving the bad times in writing isn't actually re-experiencing them. Writing about them will surprise you with forgotten details and never-before-seen connections, and this time you will have the chance to see what was going on.

    Many writers I know remain in stasis, flat-line competent, stuck because they can't go forward until they go back.

    Reliving the bad times in writing has the side effect of catharsis. Some things we can get out of our system. Sometimes the way to deal with the bad thing, to get over it, is to understand it. That happens in the writing.

- Rather than forcing yourself to revisit bad times, let them happen to someone else: a character in a story, a persona in a poem, or a masked stand-in for yourself in an essay. Try it in third

person, calling yourself "he" or "she" instead of "I." This sub-
terfuge, rather than the direct approach, not only makes writing
about the experience easier but also may be more effective in
exposing hidden truths.

- That hopeful writer afraid to strip down told me that it was
  mostly the mechanics of writing that held him back: "Working
  out the right presentation and format, i.e., working out a plot,
  personages, setting, etc., so that somebody else will want to read
  beyond the first sentence."

  This writer studied and took classes and read and read
  about the "mechanics." He knew his mechanics. The mechanics weren't his problem.

  See how he's still worried about what others will think—"so
  that somebody else will want to read"? See how he's worried
  about arranging it all ahead of time, before he's even started
  writing?

  This writer will almost certainly trivialize his most deeply
  felt material, but not from lack of skill. His focus on technique
  protects him from jumping into the sea. This guy wears SPF
  165 sunscreen.

  There is no wasting of material. So you write about it
  before you know what you're doing. So what? I rewrote, from
  scratch, the book I'd written many years ago, back when I
  didn't know what I was doing. I'm a better writer now, but
  if I hadn't recorded those details at the time, they'd have been
  lost to me.

  Skills rise to the occasion. What you want to write, what
  wants to be written, should be given its time. Maybe you'll
  revisit it later and be grateful to the previous writer you were
  when you set down those details. Or maybe you'll find that it
  was some other fear, not a technical lack, that held you back.

  Practicing scales is good. *Only* practicing scales for months
  is deadening.

  Don't wait until you're good enough. You may never be
  "good enough." So write it now.

- In later chapters we'll talk more about how to use personal
  experience and feeling in fiction, nonfiction, and poetry. Bear
  with me. For now, I tell you that your writing skills will rise to
  the occasion. I have years' worth of evidence. For now "bare"
  with me. (Sorry.)

Shoot

How can we face the blank page or screen that contains nothing—or everything?

- The fingers know. Trust them with a pencil or on a keyboard. (More on this process in the next chapter.) Don't think, just write.

- That blank page or screen isn't so pure anyway. It doesn't care if you scribble or write nonsense on it. Buy a box of crayons and a first-grade tablet. Play.

- Some writing needs to deep-sixed. Well, so? My sisters are doctors, and if they mess up, lives are at stake. I'm not performing brain surgery here. If I mess up, nobody's going to die. Sometimes we need to push through the bad writing to get to the good stuff.

- The second-best writing advice I've heard, after writer Grace Paley's "think 'true or false'" advice, came from writer Ron Carlson: "Stay at the desk," he said. When you're distracted by a text, when suddenly the cat box must be cleaned, when you need that cup of tea, stay at the desk. The distractions are you protecting yourself from you.

  Stay at the desk. What happens in the next twenty minutes, Carlson said, will break through to whatever you've resisted or avoided. Stay at the desk.

  Skills? Oh, just write it.

- In *Ghost Girl*, author Torey Hayden describes a cure for elective mutism syndrome. "All that was needed was for someone unknown to the child to come in, set up expectations immediately that the child would speak, and then provide an unavoidable opportunity to do so."

  Writers frozen by the blank page can trick themselves out of silence. You can be your own "someone unknown." When you sit down to write, write. Poet M.H. Vorse said, "The art of writing is the art of applying the seat of the pants to the seat of the chair." Write about why you're not writing. Open up the dictionary, point blindly to a word, and use it in your first sentence. A stared-at blank page only gets blanker.

- Ralph Waldo Emerson believed that "poetry was all written down before time was," that poets "hear those primal warblings and attempt to write them down."

But sometimes we mis-hear the perfect poem that already exists and "lose ever and anon a word or a verse and substitute something of our own, and thus miswrite the poem." Those of "more delicate ear" get closer to the ideal poem but it will always remain imperfect.

What emerges on our pages may never match the perfect writing we envision. Knowing this, understanding that all we can do is try to narrow the gap, allows us to write anyway, to aim the loaded pencil and fire.

Collect Frequent Flyer Miles

How can we overcome fear of failure?

- Some, afraid they won't be able to fly, remain forever with their feet mired in the earth. If they never get off the ground, they'll never crash.

   At a writers' conference, an author known for his extreme bluntness told a man who had written ten unpublished books that he should go straight to Home Depot, buy a shovel, and take up ditch digging because he would never ever sell a single word. The author told another man attending the conference that a story he'd written needed work but had promise. Both men went home discouraged.

   The man of promise gave up writing. "I came here to get discovered," he said. "I told myself that if it didn't happen, it was time to admit failure and quit." The first man might have been expected to buy a shovel and dig a hole to crawl into, but no, he showed up the next day with ten pages of a new book.

   This little anecdote is neatly allegorical, but I swear it's true. I wish I could take it further and tell you that the first man went on to write a bestselling Oprah selection soon to be a major movie. Or that he went after the author with a shovel. As far as I know, he hasn't sold a single word. I'm guessing he's still writing and maybe self-publishing and that his life is more satisfying than the quitter's.

- The act of writing is in itself flying. Write to soar, not to arrive at a destination.

- Remember that not everything we write succeeds, however success is measured. Not everything will be published, or should be.

Not everything will be admired or understood by our trusted readers. I have thick file of failed writing labeled "lame."

It takes a lot of wing-flapping practice to learn to take off. And even when we can do spins and rolls and loops, there are still times when we can't get off the ground.

How can we deal with success?

Just try me, you might be saying.

For some, though, success—prizes, publications, critical acclaim—is a destination. Once they land, the city doesn't look quite the way they expected. Or they realize it's only a layover, not a final destination.

One man, elated when his newspaper nominated him for a Pulitzer Prize, spent the next twenty years bragging about his nomination and only fribbling at writing. ("Fribble"—isn't that a great word?)

Success changes the way others see us. A college student was earning As in her literature class. When her first novel was published by a major publishing house midsemester, suddenly she was no longer the professor's darling and had to struggle for Cs. Another writer won a state arts grant and was promptly ejected from her writers' group. I've noticed that success is not infrequently followed by divorce.

Of course, not all changes are negative. It is pleasant indeed to be recognized in the bookstore.

Success changes the way we see ourselves, too. It validates us. And sometimes it scares us. What looks like the straight path to more success turns out to branch into little dirt roads where we get lost. Several writers I know found it much easier to see their first books published than their second.

We banish fear of failure and fear of success in the same ways. First, we continue to write, no matter what. Second, we turn off what one student writer called the "infernal internal editor." Third, we remember that our purpose in writing is to explore our material, to discover our truths.

The Meaning of Writer's Block

Writer's block is nothing but an "effete bourgeois affectation," said writer John Nichols, author of *The Milagro Beanfield War* and many other books. "Do bricklayers get bricklayer's block?"

But then, nobody's telling a bricklayer to jump into an abyss, either.

Writer's block is the sudden inability to write. It's a brick wall (erected, no doubt, by a nonblocked bricklayer). It can be the feeling that the wellspring has dried up. It's the blank page that stays blank. It's what writer Edward Bryant called "literary constipation." Sometimes it's sudden, sometimes it's a slow winding down, the realization that the last time word hit paper was last year. George Eliot called it the "pitiable instance of long incubation producing no chick."

What's behind writer's block?

Let me assure you, it is *not* the gods' way of telling you that you can't write.

One cause may be a habit, like workshop student Brad's, of waiting for a brilliant idea rather than just scribbling.

Sometimes a symptom is actually a cause. Editing and polishing early pages rather than going forward looks as if work is happening while you're stuck. John Steinbeck said: "Rewrite in process is usually found to be an excuse for not going on."

I get stuck when I'm trying really hard to control a story, especially its characters' behavior. That's when I let them give me a good talking-to. "It's not about what you want," they say. "What about our needs?"

Many, when they're first learning about writing techniques, are stifled by all the choices to be made as they write. This is a temporary condition. The cure is to write through it. Soon the technical considerations will be second nature, close to the intuitive way we wrote before we knew anything about craft.

Writer Ron Powers said: "Writer's block is partly a lack of courage to write badly."

Traveling home one winter, I turned off Utah's Highway 191 into Devil's Canyon, with sweet memories of camping there years ago. I wanted to find *our* campsite, and I needed a break from hours of driving. I slid along the slushy road, far enough away to park and, um, make some yellow snow.

When I started up again, the car slipped sideways. Wheels spun in the slush. I was stuck.

How stupid of you, I said to myself. *How idiotic. What were you thinking?*

I collected pine branches and jammed them under the tires. I stayed stuck.

A nice couple in a truck came upon me and tried pushing me out. I stayed stuck. They left, promising to send a tow truck, though it'd be some time before they got in the vicinity of cell phone reception.

I gave up trying to get unstuck. I put on hat and mittens and set off to find the campsite with the big rock just behind it. I swung my arms

in the high country sunshine. I saw rabbit footprints, a deer boing-
ing through drifts, and the illusion of an orange two-man tent with
a big white dog beside it. The high blue blaze of the sky shifted into
late-afternoon glow. By the time I returned to the car, the mud and
slush had frozen. I got in and drove away.

When I'm stuck on a writing problem, I work hard to solve it. I
focus on it bravely; I stay at the desk. Eventually, when nothing happens, I give up and go to the symphony or take a hike in the desert. The
writing solves its own problem in my absence. I'll be darned if I know
how. I'm only grateful. I climb back into the story and drive away.

Stop and Write

Blame writer's block on the monsters. Blame fear of jumping into the
abyss on the monsters. What fears are keeping you from truthtelling?

1. What are your monsters?
2. What writing (and life) strategies have you developed to protect yourself from your monsters?
3. What strategies can you develop to face and subdue your
   monsters?

When writer Gale Grant was my student, she wanted to write about
her experience of being a model in Paris, but she couldn't get started.
Then she wrote a couple of pages and immediately stalled. At last she
wrote this in her journal:

> At first I didn't really know what was missing, but I had that
> nagging feeling that there was something lacking. It was
> like when you leave somewhere and forget your purse or
> sunglasses. At first you feel that your hands are empty and
> then you leap to the realization that you've left something
> behind. But this missing was more than that. It wasn't
> as obvious as a possession, and it wasn't my hands that
> felt empty: it was my eyes and my heart. I kept waiting
> for the sudden realization of what was missing, the time
> when I would jump up and say, "Oh, I left, or forgot . . ."
> Weeks passed without relief from the subtle pining, and
> my sadness grew.
>
> Then it happened. I remembered sitting curled up on
> the couch, reading at my boyfriend's house in France,

when his father came in and opened the curtains. I was
at a particularly funny part of the book and was laughing
a bit hysterically and wiping tears from my eyes, when
Jean turned to me from the window, his body outlined by
the gray sky glare, and said, "Elle rit, seule." She laughs
alone. Shaking his head in mock concern, he left the
room. Tears of laughter were drying on my cheeks, but I
was overwhelmed by sorrow. I stared out the window and
tried to remember the last time I had seen sunlight. I put
my book down, forgetting to mark my place, pulled my
boots and warm jacket on, and went for a melancholy walk
through the dreary suburb and the misty forest encircling
it. I began to understand what was missing, and then I
could write my story.

Talking to herself in her journal helped Grant understand what
was holding her back. She struggled from "an utter lack of confidence" and "worry about the technical things." Third problem?
"The hardest to overcome, and the most marvelous. To delve deep
into motives without being shy or coy, without frightening myself."
Subduing her monsters and finally writing "Neon Sun" helped her
practice "how to write the truth, to delve, learn, and push away
the hypocrisy, false reasoning, the daily untruths that we surround
ourselves and others with."

Here's the opening to her story "Neon Sun":

Bar du Texas. I saw it on my way home from the casting
audition, and convinced the taxi driver to stop after only
a few blocks. "Ce n'est pas Champ du Mars, mademoi-
selle," he kept repeating.

"I know, it's okay. Okay, okay, ici c'est bien."

I stepped into the rain-filled gutter and slammed the door.

Walking back to the Bar of the Texas, I wondered what I
wanted. In French when one says I miss it or I miss you,
one literally says, it is missing from me, or you are missing
from me. Something was missing from me. I just didn't
know what it was.

The audition had been more ridiculous than usual. I had
to pretend that a frog was hopping from my hand, up my

arm, over my shoulder and into my cleavage. It was a commercial for some German brand of chocolate. What frogs and chocolate and cleavage had to do with each other would remain a mystery, as I wouldn't get the part. In fact, I hadn't gotten any jobs in over a month. They could see that something was missing.

In the Bar du Texas I shook the rain out of my hair and took a seat at the bar. I didn't order a margarita. I had been in Paris long enough to know better. A rim coated with sugar and a sweet green liquid with two flecks of ice was the best you could expect.

"A tequila and a beer. You got Lone Star?"

The bartender stared me down until I translated my order into French. He pointed to all of the tequilas in front of the mirror, shrugged, and walked away.

I turned my attention to the customers. I opened my ears for English, my eyes for tennis shoes. There were plenty of French people lined along the bar with their leather shoes, drinking dubious looking margaritas and the national favorite, Pernod and water. I watched the bartender pour a shot of tequila for a man at the other end of the bar. The bartender returned to me, and in my best French I asked for the same tequila as the man down the bar.

I had done a television commercial when I first arrived in France. The set was a very crowded bar. You see a man and a woman drinking the same brand of beer. They see each other, but the bar is so full of people that they can't reach each other. So the woman, me, climbs onto the bar and crawls along it, with the customers picking up their drinks to let her pass, the bartender gallantly wiping the bar ahead of her. I was wearing a sexy red dress. I thought about beer and cleavage. But in America, computer-animated frogs sold beer.

I'm not homesick, I told myself.

Several tequila shots later, I noticed the man had left, but that wasn't what it was. If only it were that simple. I had a

man in Paris, I even had a man in the States. I could have
any amount of men that I desired.

I had another shot, pushed my hair out of my face, and
wiped the sweat from my brow. My eyes caught for the first
time the neon sun over the bar.

The story is about, in Grant's words, "Longing for so much, for so
many impossible things, a death of romantic notions, a self-imposed
exile, and the emergence of a dubious new perspective of the world
and its inhabitants." But she knows this only now that she's faced and
come to understand the dark fears that at first didn't want the story to
see the light of the page.

Playing With Blocks

Writer's blocks are silent and invisible. They are made of fear.

Turn them into a pile of children's wooden alphabet blocks. Let
them spell out the names of the fears. Build a tower and knock it down.

Throw out all but one or two blocks. Use the scraps of remaining
fear to energize the writing.

3

JUMPING INTO THE ABYSS:
UNDERSTANDING THE CREATIVE PROCESS

Deep menacing voice: Into the woods!

Squeaky little voice: Oh no! Not the woods!

Deep and commanding: Into the woods.

Squeakier: Oh no, anything but the woods.

Deep and delighted: Annnnnnyyything?

Squeaky and resigned: The woods.

Does anybody but my sisters and me remember that junior-high recitation? We loved it, I suppose, for the scary, tantalizing implications in that drawn-out "anything." The woods were bad, but "anything" was wonderfully wicked.

Risks in writing are also frightening and exciting both. Too much fear shuts us up, but a little fear adds an edge. It acknowledges the power of our writing. It *adds* power to our writing. It intensifies the excitement.

So you take the scary, thrilling leap. Then what? How do you access your truths? How do you get to the depths? How do you get there again and again?

Me: Into the abyss!

Myself: Who, me?

Me: Into the abyss.

Myself: Easy for you to say.

Me: At least step up to the lip of the abyss.

Myself: Does our insurance cover this?

Me: Absolutely. (Hee hee) Not.

Myself: Anything but the abyss.

Me: Annnnnnyyything?

Myself: Aaaaaaiiiieeeee!

Magnetism

You are the lodestone. Once you've jumped, you'll attract details, lines of dialogue, memories, ideas, and all that the story needs. It is the process of writing that makes this magic happen.

Workshopper Joe, the writer with all those plot ideas, had a very hard time giving up his practice of planning a story. With his exhaustive character descriptions and elaborate plot outlines, he was in control. He was the god of the world of his story. He didn't want to give up that power or that safety.

Workshopper Marie knew her stories came out superficial. How could that be when she was not merely willing but downright eager to write about her most disturbing personal material? She had a hard time giving up her habit of planning, using notes such as "Chapter five will explain how my abortion at age sixteen destroyed my relationship with my husband seventeen years later," and her belief that she understood exactly what all of her experiences meant. She was the god of her project, which was to inscribe what she'd learned on tablets for the benefit of others. She didn't want to doubt anymore or give up the generous impulse to help others.

Your stories discover themselves in the writing. Writing into the unknown darkness is the process that sparks the surprises, the unexpected connections. You may be uncertain or frightened about writing your stories without the security of a plan. But to write life's truest moments, you have to learn to write into uncharted territory. Only by writing into the dark will you come to light.

Jazz pianist Keith Jarrett creates by beginning with no subject or melody in his mind: "I have to *not* play what's in my ears if there's something in my ears. I have to find a way for my hands to start the concert without me."

When it comes to creating, our hands know more than our heads.

My student Mel Carlson, who for twenty-two years ran a university's screenwriting program, gave a hooray and three cheers for my "no outline, no plotting, let the story find itself" approach to creative writing. He and the other writers in the program were "always under fire from scholars, film historians, film theorists, semioticists, semanticists, constructionists, and a few intellect-constipated graduate students . . . because we didn't provide intellectual roadmaps to writing." The writers, however, understood the necessity of folding up the map and stashing it in the glove compartment. Novelist E.L. Doctorow said, "Writing is like driving at night in the fog. You can only see as far as your headlights, but you can make the whole trip that way."

Relinquish control. From your journal, from your answers to my nosy questions in the first chapter, from your freewriting, pick up a handful of the shapeless wet clay of your material. Work it by free-associating from the most compelling images or the most mysterious lines. When it takes the form of humans, even if they're nearly in the image of their maker, grant them free will. Forget coming down from the mountain bearing commandments. Go back to the burning bush. The truths—for your stories, for yourself, and finally, for your readers—can't be reasoned out, planned, plotted, explained. The gospel according to you can't be known until you've written it.

Speaking at the Sorbonne in 1955, artist Salvador Dali set his elbows on the lecture table and proclaimed: "All emotion comes to me through the elbow." Surrealist that he was, he may have been having some fun with his audience, but I think he was on to something.

Our muscles know more than our brains. The physical act of making paintings, music, and stories, without knowing in advance what they are going to be, is what releases their truths, quite apart from our control.

I've brought in some big guns to quote—the likes of Jarrett, Doctorow, and Dali—because many will resist this next advice, and hey, it helps to have the famous on your side. So, okay, I'm not trying to start a battle, but here it is: Write by hand.

Yeah, but my hand can't keep up with my brain, my students protest.

Well, I say, slow down your brain.

Oh but revision is so much easier on the computer, they say.

Sure. Revision of the spellcheck and cut-and-paste variety: cosmetic revision. Deeper revision still needs a slow hand. And besides, I tell them, as easy as revision may be, I notice that once you've saved the document, you actually do very little of it.

Over the years, I've observed that keyboard composers tend to write slick, plot-driven stories relying on stock language, and that handwriters tend to write character-driven, fresher stories. Of course, this is a generalization and it may be unfair to assume a causal relationship, but I've learned that my own writing and my students' stories are richer and deeper when the hand, holding pencil to paper, taps into the subconscious.

James Dickey began some of his later poems by rolling a sheet of paper into his typewriter, starting with a word or an image, typing as fast as possible with no punctuation, and free-associating until he filled a single-spaced page. From this raw material he plucked out single images that seemed particularly rich and drew out thematic threads that evolved into poems. He was tapping into the subconscious, going with no agenda into the unknown, and using muscle not mind to do it.

How can you tap into your subconscious? Believe me, you can't do it by thinking. Experiment with writing by hand. Or use your keyboard the way Dickey did.

My student Ali—bright, pre-med—fought me all the way on this process. Then her roommates failed to pay the electric bill, and the power was cut off. She handed in her final story, typed up at the college's computer lab, with this note: "This story was composed on paper, handwritten in a room lit only by oil lamplight." Even without the note, I'd have recognized the writing as significantly deeper and truer than the competent, polished stories Ali had handed in before.

True confession: I've always written poems by hand, but I trained myself to write prose by efficient keyboard. I started my novel *Meridian 144*, in pre-PC days, on my Brother typewriter while I was on Guam, and in transit back to the States, my Brother died. (That doesn't sound good, does it?) I was reduced to continuing the book by hand, on my mother-in-law's kitchen table (thank you, Dorothy). There I learned that the surprises, the truths emerged when I slowed down to pencil speed. The story went below its action plot, discovered thematic depths, and surprised the heck out of me.

Big news: George Lucas, master of the *Star Wars* universe, wrote *The Phantom Menace* with No. 2 pencils. When the Dixon Ticonderoga folks found out, they sent him a whole crate of pencils.

My Brother was healed, and since then I've gone through several computers. But they are tools. They cannot do what my Blackfeet Indian pencils can do.

What process taps into your subconscious? Try using your keyboard to free-associate: fast, without judgment. Then print out your page and move to pencil. If you usually write first drafts on the keyboard, try your next draft writing by hand.

What my students write in class, on the spot, is nearly always better than what they've labored over at home. They're depressed when they see that what they wrote in a ten-minute exercise has much more life than what they worked so hard at for long hours. However, they can take the process back to the privacy of their homes and remember to stop *thinking* so much.

I like to show off my prominent writer's hump, the thick callus on the middle finger of my right hand, though it looks as if I'm giving people the finger. (Okay, maybe I am.) I need my Mac, yes, to know if my scribbled pages are cogent and potent, but I know that machines were made after the day of rest, in the second week, after true creation.

What taps out of my fingertips on a keyboard is civilized. It is neat. It clicks daintily, letting me know that real work is being executed. It is, I'm sorry, mechanical. It wants to trick me into accepting its sheen. On my screen, it is as slick as television. From my printer, it is as familiar as last week's best-seller.

I've got to be right up there among the world's fastest typists. My junior-high claim to fame was the Top Typing Award, 94 words per minute, no errors, on a manual yet (while all around me were cheerleaders and pep squad presidents). They don't call me Fingers Files for nothing, but typing requires my second hand, and I think I'm smart enough to recognize a double meaning when I see one.

What emerges from my yellow pencil applied to paper is first-hand. It is inchoate creation, nonsense, blue-footed boobies and scarlet-rumped mandrills and wadded up first drafts in which kittens have handles and humans have no elbows. It is a mess. It is the beginning that is the word, and then it crosses out the word and draws an arrow to a new word and crosses that out and then circles it and writes in *stet*. It lifts its paper surface and swims in the black unformed vapor, where it finds what does not hide in machines—forgotten scraps of memory, hearts that swell with oxygen-rich complexity.

Art is not premeditated. It has learned its moves, it can draw the human body, it can do fugues and sonnets, until it knows them in its muscles. And then it can forget its moves. Art is stupid muscle, brain disengaged, the hand goofing around on the page. The mindless hand dips below the page and scoops up a swimming mess of memories and other people's truths and imagined flotsam. And the paper becomes a slide. And art looks through the microscope at the magnified swarm and makes connections. Where does art come from? It is the truth that nothing but the blind pencil on the paper knows.

You want answers? Me and my Mac have 'em. You want the hard, deep questions? They're in the heart, they're pumped through the body—yes, and the brain—and sometimes my hand curled around a pencil catches and releases them.

You want rationality? Inquire of your microchips. You want art? Ask your muscles.

Gravity

Writing about your personal pains and passions, in spite of fears, is a big risk. Writing into the unknown is a big risk. So once you've jumped, you might as well let gravity have its way. No grabbing onto branches protruding from the cliffside. No opening the parachute. Going all the way means taking some additional risks:

- When the writing wants to go off on a tangent, let it. When a detail you can't explain lands on the page, let it stay. When another voice shouts to be heard, let it take over.

  Occasionally these moves turn out to be false. The next draft can remove them.

  Nearly always, though, you'll find out why they intruded. The tangent may be the real story, or it may be a dirt-road side trip that gives new meaning to the eventual return to the blacktop. The surprise detail reappears later in the story, and you discover what you were, unbeknownst to yourself, setting up. The loud voice belongs to someone bouncing in the chair, hand up: *Me, me! Call on me! Ooh ooh! I know the answer!* And it does. The loud voice is supplanting a wimpy voice.

- When you get to a scene that's going to be tough to write, write it anyway. Perhaps you don't know how to handle it. Perhaps you don't know what's going to happen in it. You tell yourself, *I'll just skip that puppy for now and write it later*.

  This invisible scene is crucial to the story. It can't be written and inserted later on. Write into its blankness, make it visible, and you will discover how everything that follows depended on it.

- Make bad things worse. We grow fond of the people in our stories, and we want to protect them, to grant them good lives and happiness, to give them their hearts' desires. But they're in trouble, or they have bad personalities, or nobody loves them. They're making bad choices. They wouldn't be in the story if something wasn't wrong.

  Don't send them to therapy. Don't kiss their boo-boos and make them all better. Don't bring on the handsome stranger to sweep them into love and a clean credit record.

  They're slow learners. They're messed up. They need to hit bottom before they can pick themselves up and dust themselves off. You want to intercede and ease the way, but like any other humans, they need to solve their own problems. Grant them salvation, in the end, but send them to hell first.

- Keep your eyes open. Some details and events will be as unsavory as a dead monkey. It's tempting to protect readers (and ourselves) by sanitizing, by prettifying the material—spray cologne on the critter and pin a bow on its head—or by ignoring it altogether. However, the distortion or denial of the truth to render it inoffensive makes for phony stories. And it doesn't bring the monkey back to life, either.

  Director Akira Kurosawa said, "To be an artist means never to avert your eyes."

- Bless mixed feelings. When the writing gets untidy and convoluted, resist the inclination to tame it. Risk incoherence. Poet Seamus Heaney maintained that poetry is meant to complicate experience, not simplify it. Sell platitudes to a greeting card company, but allow nuance and emotions too complex to have names to lead your stories far and deep and upside down.

  A sign in front of a row of apartments announced: Complex Yard Sale. You know I had to stop.

- Boldly go. "How do you know a good writer when you see one?" a writers' conference participant asked Robley Wilson, editor of *North American Review* from 1969 to 2000. He answered simply: "A good writer has an authoritative voice." No reader wants to go where no man has gone before with a nervous tour guide. Writers who are going where indeed many have gone before (virtually impossible not to) have only boldness to make their stories new.

- Get strange. In the introduction to *The Best American Short Stories* 1995, editor Jane Smiley discussed her choices. "Certain words reappear in my descriptions of these stories: 'strange,' 'exotic,' 'rich,' 'charming.' Finally the thing that all good short stories offer is a sudden and ineluctable experience of something not ourselves, a character, an incident, a place more or less distant from who and where we are that is, for a few minutes, so much more alluring than what we know that we give ourselves over to it."

  Among her selections was "Hand Jive," by writer Andrew Cozine, a story about a boy with strange compulsions. Cozine says that he'd started writing about his odd childhood friends, "but once I'd started writing about my own odd ways, I couldn't stop."

  Stories can be strange in various ways: including content, language, technique, and voice. See Lorrie Moore's stories in *Bark* for examples of all of these—and for inspiration to be strange in your own writing ways. But strangeness can hardly be planned. When it comes knocking, open the door a crack and let it sneak in. You may fear it will never leave, but it will. Then next week, its cousin will show up. Or so you can only hope.

- Take the right risks. Stories that are all clever technique may be interesting experiments or puzzles but they're just showing off. They end up contrived instead of startling and new. Stories that set out to shock, for shock's sake, end up distressing (or tedious) rather than disturbing.

  It's tricky to seek risk for its own sake, Evel Knievel style. The main thing is the willingness to take risks when the chance appears, leaping canyons when you've driven full speed right up to the brink.

  Risks with language, technique, and form might be avoidance of the real risk: the material itself. Poet Donald Hall talked about the poet's need to live with the volume turned up in order to receive strong material. Yes, we need a strong cage—solid technique—but, Hall explained, "a strong cage is nothing if there is no lion inside it. One kind of bad poem makes a strong cage with bars two inches thick and heavy wire between the bars, and inside the cage there is only a little bunny rabbit going hippity-hop. This bunny is an evasive lion—or a lion with the volume turned down."

Bait

Used to be, I couldn't write without my cat reposing on my desk. Simon might have posed for Jim Davis when he drew fat, striped, grumpy, pizza-loving Garfield, and he didn't merely sprawl but repose. He was my muse, and he was not averse to the role. Most cats, I believe, are muses of the literary arts and are naturally attracted to books and pencils and paper.

Simon served me well for many years, but—you've guessed the end of this—he grew old and died. I buried him outside Mobridge, South Dakota, in a shoebox with a copy of James Dickey's poem "The Heaven of Animals."

At first I approached my Simon-less desk nervously, afraid I'd write only uninspired words or nothing at all. However, household cats, though they may inhabit the heaven of animals, are allowed to visit their people, and sometimes I caught sight of his apparition as it flitted around a corner or when I tripped on it.

Your particular muse, whether creature or object, no doubt serves, as Simon did for me, to ferry you away from your desk with its pencil sharpener and paper clips and erasers and screen into the land of imagination and memory. And such was the service of the original cast of muses, too.

The nine Muses were the daughters of Zeus, Lord of the Sky, and Mnemosyne, Memory. The results of this union should surprise no one. "He is happy whom the Muses love," wrote Hesiod. "For though a man has sorrow and grief in his soul yet when the servant of the Muses sings, at once he forgets his dark thoughts and remembers not his troubles. Such is the holy gift of the Muses to men."

He's describing the creative process, when the writer, transported by imagination and memory, is hardly aware of the desk and the keyboard. It's interesting that we need to embody that process—women, cats—perhaps to be sure we can lure it back. What is your talisman?

Here, Kitty Kitty Kitty

How can you invite your muse to make regular visits?

- Don't wait for it to come calling. If I waited for inspiration, I'd write three poems and one and a half stories a year. It's not that I dislike writing, though there are many who prefer having written to actually writing. Like many others, once I'm at the desk, all is well in my world, but sometimes I have to kick myself in the seat of the pants to get there. You can seriously wrench your back doing that.

So, no excuses. The cat box may need cleaning, the yard raking, the email checking. If you succumb to duty, no pride of accomplishment will follow, only the queasy knowledge of loss.

- Don't wait until you have enough time. Time is both the cheapest and the most valuable coin in your pocket, and you will never have enough. What does it cost? If you don't have two hours, take twenty minutes. Take what you can, as often as you can. What is it worth? Your writing life.

  Many who want to write are waiting until their lives are cleared of clutter—kids, jobs, committees, litter boxes. *When the youngest starts school . . . when I retire, then I'll write*. Or maybe when they're dead, then they'll write.

  Those who do take up writing at long last find they've got years of catching up to do. The desire to write doesn't translate immediately into skill.

  "I write when I'm inspired," said writer Peter DeVries, "and I see to it that I'm inspired at nine o'clock every morning."

- To lure new kitty Paka, the wannabe calico, to my desk or lap, I simply use the universal pet language of the triple pat, accompanied by embarrassing attempts to speak their language more directly. To lure my writing muse, I sit down at my desk and sharpen several pencils. Because I've trained it well, it has a Pavlovian response to the smell of fresh graphite and shows right up.

  I hear many successful writers exhort hopeful writers to write every day. I don't quite believe them when they insist, ahem, it is their own practice. The exhortation convinces those who don't do four hours or ten pages a day, or whatever goal has been set, that they're not real writers.

  Regular writing, with vacations allowed, *is* important. For some, writing at the same time of day is important.

  If you think you're not a real writer (whatever that is) because you missed a day or three, remember that irregular rewards are even more effective in training than absolutely consistent reinforcement.

  No job description exists except the one we write for ourselves.

Care, Feeding, and Training

Muses require behavioral conditioning. What practices will help train yours?

- The more you work with your muse (i.e., the more you work), the more readily you can summon it.

- Muses often prefer clear, clean, private workspaces. Now I have an office, but once my mother-in-law Dorothy's kitchen table sufficed. I don't understand coffeehouse writing, but apparently it works for some. Perhaps you live in a city with a library or literary center that offers study rooms or writing space.

   You may find that you're most able to lose yourself in writing when you're alone at your desk or anonymous among others also scribbling away. I learned how much I need solitude when a colleague doing a study about writing asked if he could observe me at work. He said he would stay in the background, totally unobtrusive. My immediate reaction was: Absolutely not, I don't know you that well, that's way too intimate.

   Finally, I let him do it. He sat silently at the back of the room, and I sat at my desk, noisily grinding down pencils. Write a line. Sharpen. Write a line. Sharpen. Put on the Mahler CD that saw me through the last story. Sharpen. Write a line. Sharpen. (Later he told me that I wiggle my toes when I write. Thanks for sharing that.) At last I gave up and faked it by retyping pages I'd already written.

   Your muse wants to transport you into the world of your story. Self-consciousness sinks your feet deep into the muddy world of beholders, judges, editors, and moms.

   Find a room of your own. Or a late-night kitchen table of your own.

- Figure out a reverse rhythm method. What regular pattern will encourage (rather than avoid) fertilization?

   I begin each day's writing session by typing into the computer what I wrote by hand the previous day. This gets my hands in motion and returns me to the story's world.

   Then I continue by hand. At the end, I make a couple quick notes about what the next day's episode might be.

   What pattern will call forth your muse? What rhythm ripens the page for conception? Oh dear, I'm in over my head with this metaphor. You know what I mean.

- Prepare for glory. You cannot force brilliance. You cannot will enlightenment. All you can do is get ready, be receptive, and hope.

  Preparation means reading. And reading. And reading. The writers I know are reading addicts. I'm always surprised—don't know why, since it happens every semester—when hopeful writers confess they don't read, and I wonder what impulse drives their desire. (Some fear the influence of other writers on their work, a fear that should be disregarded, but that's another matter.) Reading lets us know what's been done already so we can make our retelling of the old stories somehow new. Reading tunes our ears to language, pacing, technique, so we learn by both osmosis and conscious attention. Reading is not duty, though, for us writers. It's the way we breathe.

  Preparation means learning craft. Writing is a series of choices: this word, that word, this line break or another, a comma or not. In the beginning, the choices are intuitive and we're hardly aware we're making choices at all. When writers take classes and read books about technique, the new awareness of all those choices and considerations and effects and dos and don'ts can make writing feel stilted and difficult. That's a necessary stage, and the only way past it is through it, until writing is once again intuitive but with the solid ground of craft beneath it. Warning: You'll go through this once but, I'm sorry, it's not over. It's a cycle because we learn more all the time, master it, and then learn more. I'm not sorry, really, because this is the way to glory. We climb, we slide, we climb again, and there is no end. Hallelujah.

Bring on the Catnip

Sometimes the muse needs a wink and a giggle. You can borrow teases from other writing books or invent your own, it doesn't matter. The idea is to come at the material sideways, to surprise it into the light, even if you didn't know what the material was. Any game you play to get the pencil into motion will do it. (Or, sometimes not. Well, so what?) *Play* is the word of the moment here.

- Open your dictionary at random. Write down the two words at the top of the far right and far left columns. Check out their meanings if you wish—or not. Write using these two words in the first paragraph. Joint bar and juba, zinc and zowie, redemption and reel, hack and haircloth, subversively and sugar, wanderer and warp. Use the random words to entice your muse.

- Make up a totally outrageous first line, knowing you're never going to write the actual story. Here's a model: "As Gregor Samsa awoke one morning from uneasy dreams, he found himself transformed in his bed into a gigantic insect." Top that famous Kafka line.

- Write an apologetic note to attach by magnet to your refrigerator.

- Write about the most important thing you've had, but lost.

- Open your dictionary, close your eyes, and zap your pencil down. Open your eyes, write down the nearest word. Repeat four times. Write, working in these five words.

- Write a paragraph in the voice of a ghost.

- Write a letter to someone in today's news. To the reporter stuck in the elevator at the NFL preseason opener. To the idiot who wrote the comment about the surrogate mother pregnant with twins. To the woman robbed at gunpoint when she stopped to move large rocks blocking the road. You get the idea.

- Write two paragraphs following your outrageous first line. No cockroaches, please. (You'll find that once you're writing, many of these exercises will grow beyond the suggested limit. Who are you to stop them?)

- Finish this sentence and see what follows: The question I wish someone would ask me is . . .

- Open your closet. Inside is your alter ego, and it is not happy. What does it say?

   This exercise was suggested by poet Gina Franco's notes about hearing a voice: "I was putting shoes in my closet and I was worrying, and I heard—really heard—this little voice yelling at me. I stood there, in front of my closet, stunned. I know how trite this sounds, how pop psychology, but this really happened. . . . It was as if I'd been ventriloquizing this little voice that had been screaming at me all this time, this little demon who'd been acting out to try and get my attention, and of course I hadn't been listening because I'd been giving all that energy away. So I sat down with a notebook and wrote down some of the things this voice had to say, and boy was she pissed."

The resulting poem, "The Spirit That Appears When You Call," published in *Crazyhorse*, scared Franco to pieces in the writing. "And yet," she said, "what an amazing thing to actually listen directly to this voice, this muse, who is so strong-willed, self-assured, and self-centered, demanding, complex. We always say that the poem is smarter than we are, and I have always sensed the truth of that while writing, but now I know that I'm not in control of things. *She* is, whoever she is. And she's absolutely smarter than I am. I'm a silly idiot, compared. I'm just listening in."

The voice that yells or maybe whispers at you when you open that forbidden door may scare you, too. Don't analyze it or judge it. Just let it speak. Write down what it says, in its own voice.

- There's a childhood experience you want to write about but you aren't sure how to approach it. Write a title at the top of a page: The Tree, Chloe's Death, Button Box, whatever will label it for you. Now call up or text three friends. Say, "No time for chitchat, just give me a word." Back at your page, use the three magic words you've been given in the paragraphs or stanzas that follow your title.

Another piece of Gina Franco's came from this random-word exercise. This poem, the story of a childhood, grew from that simple exercise:

Velvet

But inside her, there is always velvet,

velvet with its give and yield, the kind you

find at a pet store, a bin full of long

ears and noses busy snuffing up nerves

among the cedar chips and their eyes

opening wide as if rabbits couldn't know

what softness brings, as if they'd never know

the smell of something long stored away now

brought into light, and now too her mother

with a camera pointing at her, red

child on the lap of the Easter rabbit,

softness of the body hiding inside

the costume, eyes glinting from the wide holes

in the mask not a single sobbing breath

of wind down the trail of mesquite and broom

foot-printing the hills of some rancher's land.

The bird dog lifts his ears to the sound

of velvet, the girl listens to the drawn

cries of a crow, her father walks

with the silence of the shotgun, waiting

for the pointer to find scent, the rabbit

at the end of it blinking, its wide eyes

shrinking from the scuffle of their feet like

velvet settling, laid over lines, drying

across the ceiling of an uncle's garage

where they talk inside the smell of salted

skin. At least three dollars for each good pelt

he says, and they scream like children when,

sleeves rolled down his forearms, he brings

the club down on their heads, saving

their feet for cheap key chains, for luck

that softness doesn't seem to have inside

of cages, chicken wire, tubes of water,

and sometimes boys who try kicking the cage

around to see what happens to velvet

tumbling. And, in the after quiet,

she bites the hands reaching toward her, so they

stone her, they open her belly and pull

some things out, open the pink albino

eye and groan at the fluid inside. Then they

bury the carcass without thinking first

of washing their sticky hands in the sink

before eating dinner, before setting

the table, in the still softness of her

beige room, she sits on the carpet picking

at the velveteen of Bunny's stuffed neck,

the rabbit's eyes dull with scratches, eyes left

behind on her bed at night when she stands

in the hall, hearing her father breathe in his room

in the darkness, on the futon, kicking

off the sheets. Awake from a fluid dream

of a woman's eyes staring from behind

a gag, her white skin settling in fat pools

around her, naked, bald. And a man's

voice said, *this is your rabbit*, so she woke

to this dream inside her, with his teeth wrapped

in her hair, and his hands inside her thighs

where he fingered her coldly. But it has

always been like this—wild, insidious,

and commanding because she gives to it,

fascinated by it and caught by it,

as velvet only listens and is quiet.

"Velvet" was the trigger word to elicit the details and the pictures that spiral one to the next and circle back, the associations and implications underneath that reveal the little girl's story. The other words? I doubt that even Franco remembers what they were or knows if they made the final cut. The muse took the offered bait, and that's what matters.

What word or image will trigger your subconscious? Don't answer that, for you can't know in advance. The material's there, below the surface, waiting to be tapped into. It isn't some single right word that is required as probe. All you need is the willingness to play at the exercises and to listen to your closeted voices. Open the door and let them speak.

4

WILLING THE FLESH:
APPLYING METHODS OF STRONG STORYTELLING

Isolation. Rejection. Divorce. Loneliness. Poverty. Childlessness. Guilt. Loss of mother, of father. War. Childhood abuse. Illness. Death of the beloved. Psychological trauma. The death of a child. And love, in all its varieties: of pets, of mountains, of music, of parents, of monsoon storms, of brothers and sisters, of vocation, of friends, of gardens, of books, of lovers, of _____, and of _____.

You can fill in the blanks to label your own most intense emotional, physical, spiritual, psychological experiences.

Whatever they are, our most powerful emotions and experiences lead to our best writing. But writing about our personal, private intensities also leads to problems writers willing to take additional risks need to confront. The willingness to face the material, to let the process of writing discover the truth, and to take it deep—yes, good, you're there. Your spirit is willing. Now let the flesh also be willing. The next step is to practice approaches and techniques for making your stories strong for the reader.

How can we present our emotionally intense material so that others also feel the intensity?

The writer's biggest challenge is to make the writing live up to the power of the experience and the emotion that inspired it. Or to come as close as we can, anyway.

Workshop student Marie was ready to spill it all. Her life was an open book. Horrors untold would now be told. So why weren't her readers moved? Why weren't they charged to take up the cause? She tried nonfiction. She tried fiction. In desperation, she tried a poem. The problem, it seemed, had nothing to do with genre.

Direct spillage is rather like an overturned truck. The driver is unhurt, but all over the highway are those live chickens or milk or fertilizer or pork parts. It's a nuisance and a mess, it slows traffic and attracts flies. It's a picture in the newspaper. But we know the driver survived. It's a curiosity, not a tragedy.

With writing, we also know the driver survived, or we wouldn't have the testimony. Nothing to be done about that. But I suggest that spilling the guts directly across the page is the major impediment to affecting anyone but the driver. If you're famous, curiosity may be enough. The rest of us writers must promise and come through with the details, the secrets, the nuances of the truths since no one else knows them.

Readers do not feel our emotions because we tell them to. It is not enough to talk about an experience. So how do we get beyond an abstract label to a re-creation of the experience?

Whatever pleasures and pains you'd put on your own list would be no more profound or moving to readers than the abstractions that began this chapter. The word "divorce" might call up memories if you've been touched by divorce, but if not, the label elicits no more than a head shake. So first, the way to evoke feelings in your readers is to re-create the situations that led to *your* intense feelings in the first place. That means naming names. That means calling by name.

Language Matters

To some people, words are nails to hammer a sentence together, to pound down a statement. To others, words are bubbles that look pretty and float away the hot air inside them. However, probably like you, I suffer a word lust so rampant that no book or cereal box is safe from me.

I love words. I love body words: muscle, sinew, blood. I love color words: indigo, cadmium. I love words for their sounds, the way they purse my lips and send my tongue to the back of my teeth and the roof of my mouth: leather, painted, dusk, button. I read the dictionary. I mean, just open it up and sit and read. Where else would you learn that the maypop is the edible fruit of the passion flower or that a clowder is a collection of cats?

Words are embodiment. In the beginning was the word. I loved it when Captain Picard on his Enterprise said, "Make it so." I think maybe Adam, charged with naming the creatures, was actually their creator. I imagine all the creatures swarming in the vapor, a mass of legs and beaks and wings and tentacles, all furry and scaled. And our man strides right up (he *can*—he has a name). "Octopus!" he says. "Puppy dog! Ghost-faced bat!" (And he speaks our lovely English.) He points his chubby finger at God. Make it so.

Luckily, my husband shares my word lust. I may have fallen in love with him when, the first time I had dinner with his parents, he passed me the French fries and said, "Here, have some fat sticks." Ah! At last a man who called things by name. Even now he writes "real poo" instead of shampoo on the grocery list. "Don't want any of that fake stuff," he says.

To tell your strong stories, you need strong language—that is, honest language. Search not for the clever, the fancy, or the pretty words, but for those that will make your readers see just what you see.

Honest language is often simple and direct. Which of these phrases makes a picture in your mind: a tabescent youth in a marine vessel or a thin boy in a boat? Honesty in language means finding the precisely right words for the scenes you want to draw on the page. It means naming names.

Names do count. As children we chanted: Sticks and stones may break my bones, but names will never hurt me.

Oh yeah?

We all remember the time we were called a name: sissy or loser or freak or crybaby. And we remember that pain in a way we can't remember the particular pain of the time we broke an arm. Names are seared permanently onto our hearts.

We name things that don't even require names. Cars, for instance. My husband once owned the Red Witch. When we lived in the South Pacific, we drove the Guam Bomb. And, um, why do men (and women) name the body parts they own and love? I mean, the Griffin, Little Fred, the Lovemeister, Moby Dick?

What's *in* a name? A rose by any other name would *not* smell as sweet. What's the first thing an inventor does? Not file for a patent. No. The inventor *names* the new thing. These days, the inventor hires a high-priced consulting firm. The name's important. Would you rather drive something called an Edsel or a Mustang?

Writer Madeleine L'Engle said: "To love is to call by name." In the heat of passion, we don't want to hear "Oh baby, oh baby." We want our own name whispered in our ear or cried out.

In some cultures, the true name is secret and to reveal it is to give power. Sometimes people in transition will change their names, as if that will change their identity. I know a stern woman who changed her name from Ethel to Chiffon. And damned if she isn't fluffier. Of course, it may be the new hairdo, too. I was happy to call my student Edward by the name of Mary, as requested, and I am convinced that confidence in identity translated directly to confidence as writer.

Truth is in the specifics. Any politician or bad writer can push the cry-now button with abstractions. All I have to do is say "breakup" or "run-over puppy" or "soulmate" and there is an automatic (and generic) reaction. But the words that truly move your readers are not the generic lines inside greeting cards. They are the words that are so specific, they are arrows flying in formation straight into the heart.

When it comes to love, what would we rather hear?

> Sweetheart, I'll love you 'til the end of time
>
> Your dear heart completes my rhyme.

(That's the famous poet Anonymous.)
Or this:

> . . . If I meet
>
> you suddenly, I can't
>
> speak—my tongue is broken;
>
> a thin flame runs under
>
> my skin; seeing nothing,
>
> hearing; only my own ears
>
> drumming, I drip with sweat:
>
> trembling shakes my body

(That's from "He Is More Than a Hero," written in the seventh century B.C. by Sappho, translated by Mary Barnard.)

Anonymouses never sweat, do they?

What about the terrible grief of a child's death? Here's one Julia Moore, writing about "Little Libby" in 1876:

> One more little spirit to Heaven has flown,
>
> To dwell in that mansion above.
>
> Where dear little angels, together roam,
>
> In God's everlasting love.

Oh, but here is a Japanese poet, Chiyo (1703–1775), writing of the death of her young son:

> The dragonfly hunter—
>
> today, what place has he
>
> got to, I wonder …

This haiku chokes me up as no little angels moving into sky mansions ever could.

Sometimes you can get around an abstraction by making a metaphor. The specific comparison embodies the abstraction—makes a body for it. It just doesn't cut it to say, "Well, it appears you're taking a somewhat minor problem and expanding it." No. We need to see it, so we say, "Don't make a mountain out of a molehill." Or, better, invent your own fresh metaphor: "That's just a leaky faucet, not Niagara Falls." "His guilt at breaking his diet turned a single Twinkie into an entire sheet cake." And we like to give texture to our abstractions: It's not just a big deal, it's a big *hairy* deal. Our mothers weren't going to be merely upset when we messed up as kids. They were going to have a cow, which, you've got to admit, is a lot more visual.

In choosing your words, be bold. Language that softens things up for the reader (or for the writer) can't capture your strong scenes. Euphemism is a kind of timidity that excludes access. Some clean up the fact of death by writing that people "pass away." A pediatrician told me that when she was in medical school, they didn't say patients were near death; instead, they "crumped." Sometimes humans need the easing of euphemism, but writers require the hard words that define reality.

Words are all we have.

Yes, I want to shake out a fat dictionary and roll in its lovely spilled words. Yes, I love the English language in my mouth and on my page. But as sensuous and textured and lovely as it is in all its specificity, for writers it is not dessert. It is our red meat and fish—our protein. It is our broccoli and carrots, and it gives us green life and clear sight. It is our bread, our sustenance, and our substance.

When you write, you are Adam naming genus and species. With honest, plain, clear—and sometimes surprising or soaring—language, you touch memory and make it live again for readers.

I Feel Your Pain

Every pain feels unique to the sufferer. When acquaintances say, "I know just how you feel," and politicians insist, "I feel your pain," the sufferers would laugh if it didn't hurt so much. Nobody else knows the particulars of their misery.

Yet they seek out the bookstore's self-help section and the Internet and support groups hoping others *do* know. A woman who was widowed at a young age told me how her grief was intensified because she felt all alone in it. All the books were about old people coping with widowhood. She decided to write the book she wished she would find.

Writers are faced with the paradox of describing their unique experiences, what nobody else can know, and simultaneously hoping to speak to (and for) others who have suffered in the same way. But the paradox illuminates an artist's truth. Neva Daniel, a wise teacher, explained it this way: "We move down into the well of individuality to, finally, a wellspring or stream of universality."

So don't worry about whether readers will identify with your experiences. Don't even try to find ways to give them universal appeal. Tell your own story in all its precise and lonely detail, and your readers will feel your pain.

The Truth Is in the Details

Readers are likely to be moved by your story if they're convinced of its authenticity. And the way to convince them is to offer graphic details. We believe details. The teenager knows Mom will guess the real story—that she spent the evening parked with her boyfriend—if she tells her, "Oh me and some dudes just hung out." So she tosses off: "Sherry got her dad's Camry, and he and her and Jamila went to Pat's Drive-In, you know, over on Grande, and had chili dogs and Diet Cokes, and Jamila had her hair cut weird . . ." Mom rolls her eyes, but she believes.

The insider details—what goes on in the back room of the fast-food joint, the smell of your pillow, the father who tells his son "pull my finger" and then farts, the neighbors' fights—these are what bring stories to life. Your story will jump off the page, full of vitality, when you write in the fine and intimate details.

Show, don't tell. We've all heard the advice. And it's good advice. As you get started, you may have trouble playing out fully developed scenes on the page, especially when you're writing from personal experience. After all, you already know what happened. One writer I worked with used to own and manage a sleazy motel. When he used a motel as the setting for a novel, he didn't offer the reader any details or inside information about running a motel and instead resorted to descriptions such as, well, a sleazy motel. As a reader, I was just dying to learn the secrets.

As you gain experience and learn about scenes, though, details may overwhelm you. How do you know when to go into full detail?

How Do You Know Which Details to Include?

Often the more I play out a scene in a story, the farther I get from the end. I remind myself to let the process direct the story, though it seems I'll end up with a trilogy if I keep going. I can't know, in the writing, which details belong, which ones may not finally belong but lead to details I wouldn't otherwise have known, and which ones will need a line drawn through them. So, first, I put 'em all in.

- Some writers hoard their details, cautiously saving some for the next rainy story. Details should be freely spent. There will be more. I promise.

  Sometimes we have to try out a certain detail until it shows us where it really belongs. A poetry editor accepted a poem out of a batch of mine with a note: "Good poems, but what's with all the mercury vapor lights?" How embarrassing. I hadn't even noticed the repetition of the image, which had finally found its home in the accepted poem.

- The second (or third or fourth) draft will tell you which details must remain. "Nothing is less real than realism," said artist Georgia O'Keefe. "Details are confusing. It is only by selection, by elimination, by emphasis, that we get at the real meaning of things."

  Which details build the world of your story? Which will make readers believe in that world? Which details suggest the texture of the experience? Which bring scenes to vivid life? Which details reveal who the story's cast members are in their hearts? Keep these details. Keep them all.

  Which details are irrelevant space fillers? Which function merely to get the story's people from one place to the next? As in: *The alarm woke Jake at 6:30, he shut it off, he lifted the covers off and swung his legs over the side of the bed, and then he padded down the hall* (barefoot people in stories always pad down the hall) *to the bathroom where he peed and shook, and brushed his teeth and spat in the sink, and after he put on his socks and underwear and shirt and pants and shoes, descended to the kitchen and ate a bowl of cereal and rinsed the dish, and outside unlocked the car and got in and turned the key in the ignition. . . .*

  Everyone is exhausted by the time Jake gets to the office, where the real story begins.

One of the trickiest problems is merely getting the poor guy from one place to the next. The neat solution is to skip it and simply activate your transporter. Your man will rematerialize wherever you need him.

Traveler's advisory: Beware of transportation. Sometimes the journey is the story. Often airplanes and cars are mere vehicles to get your man from one place to the next. They provide him with time to reminisce on his way to Grandpa's funeral about his great (or horrid) times with Grandpa, and thus fill readers in on more background than they need, at least before the real story is in motion.

- Every detail is significant, in some small or major way. Sometimes we include some quirky detail or character description that we're quite proud of but that misleads readers. If you include a cross-eyed chimp, there'd better be a good reason.

  Sometimes we give names to bit players rather than relegating them to "the man leaning out of the second-floor window" or "the woman singing along to the music in her earbuds." Names mean those folks are going to reappear, and readers take note and wait. (And wait.)

- Similarly, repetition of a word, image, or detail implies significance. It may take other readers to point out the repetitions you've written into the story, so subconscious is the writing process. Or when you read the story aloud, you may notice. Pay attention to those repetitions. Query yourself. What was *that* all about? Maybe it was a mercury vapor lamp looking for a home. Maybe it was mere accident. But often something you couldn't plan was at work. What was it? Should it be teased a bit closer to the surface?

  The editor of *Meridian 144* pointed out my frequent repetitions of the word "cotton." It was news to me. I did a search of the whole manuscript. Wow. Surely that wasn't an accident. What was that about? I noticed that the word often connected with Kitty's Midwestern childhood and suggested summer innocence. She wore cotton underpants and slept in cotton babydolls. I kept those repetitions, but when the word worked against the evocation of innocence, I dressed her in silk or left her undressed, so to speak.

- Writers who understand the power of detail sometimes have trouble working it in. *Deirdre entered the room with a flourish.*

She had a Rubenesque figure, little feet encased in Chinese slip-pers, and a long nose. Also a large mole at the side of her mouth. She wore a yellow silk sari with a roll of flesh showing below the blouse, both ears were pierced three times, and a butterfly tat-too graced her left shoulder. Oops, I'm almost liking this bad example. The point is, though, that clumping up descriptive details is clumsy (or humorous, whether that was the intent or not).

How can you work details in unobtrusively?

Try making them part of the scene's action: *Deirdre strutted into the room and twirled around in her yellow silk sari, triple sets of earrings chiming. She pulled the scarf from her shoulder to brandish a butterfly tattoo.*

Spread details out and balance them with dialogue and action: *Deirdre entered the room with a flourish. She was wear-ing a yellow silk sari and a roll of flesh showed below the blouse. "Hello, all," she said, "check out the new adornment." She pulled aside her scarf to reveal a butterfly tattoo on her left shoulder.*

Focus on one or two details rather than giving the exhaus-tive list: *Deirdre's large body was wrapped in a yellow silk sari, and her tiny feet were encased in Chinese slippers.*

Best of all, make details part of the narrator's observations or reactions: *Here Deirdre came in her yellow silk sari and three sets of earrings and butterfly tattoo. Always the drama queen.*

The natural details, unlike my artificial examples, will show themselves where they are needed. Trust them to work them-selves unobtrusively into your scenes.

- I wish I had a quarter for every time my students (and I) have been told to avoid repeating a word. Find a synonym, they're told. Repetition is bad. Bad, bad, bad. (Oops.) The results of this advice are ludicrous. *At the beach, Angelica watched the waves. She stood upon the billowing strand and remembered the ship to Italy when she was a child. The briny ocean crashing against the bank carried her back to that vessel she'd sailed as a stripling.* Yuck.

  What are the precise words to evoke the picture in your mind? Find them and use them. And call upon them again. Nobody's paying me that quarter, so you might as well trust your own true words and prevent a serious case of thesau-rusitis. I've seen some bad cases, and they are pretty, way too pretty.

- Oh, the power of the meaningful look. The power of silence.
    He: Hey, want to go to that new show this weekend?
    She: Well, um . . .
    Or how about:
    She: Do you still love me?
    He: Well, um . . .

    Sometimes the power of our stories comes more from what we don't say than from what we do, from the understated and the unstated. Writer Reg Sanger offered this simple advice: Never explain. Trust your details and trust what you *don't* say to layer stories.

    The page is the surface. Whether it's linear or convoluted, smoothly subtle or white-capped wild, the page is the surface. Above are hundreds of miles of atmosphere and below is the Mariana Trench. Every bit of dialogue and detail on the page is suggestive and revealing of the unspoken heights and depths. It may feel safer and necessary to spell everything out, but that's just skimming along on the surface. It may be disturbing and frightening to suggest rather than to state. Who knows what sunless creatures lurk in the depths, what cold helium beings dwell in the exosphere? If we bring them up or down to the lit surface, we can tame them and analyze them and diminish them. But when we suggest the story's subtext, we reveal the complexities. Deepening and heightening is what happens between the lines: It's the way to say the unsayable.

Tell, Don't Show

Does every word need to be flinty? Must we always avoid a nice pliable adjective? Can we never simply state something? It's easy to get carried away with the "show, don't tell" dictum.

- Minor facts probably should just be set on the page directly. "She grew up in the Midwest" doesn't require a scene of soybean fields and picket fences to demonstrate it. "He hated doing dishes" doesn't need to be illustrated with the guy resentfully scrubbing away at the sink. A piece of background information takes on misleading significance when it gets the attention of detail.

- Some facts or events don't rate full-blown scenes to show them. Still, it's possible to summarize in detail. Here, for example, is part of a sentence from Pam Houston's story "The Whole Weight of Me": "It was an East Coast story, full of lawyers and therapists and a botched custody agreement, an ex-wife who snatched a little boy out of a car seat and left thirty-minute rants on the answering machine . . ." Say no more.

- Sometimes what might look like telling is really an overheard thought, which is another way of showing. In Gale Grant's story "Neon Sun," Grant doesn't shoulder her way into the story and explain that Kate was homesick. Instead, we get this, in Kate's voice: "I'm not homesick, I told myself." Small difference, but a big difference. Later on, Kate is cross, but Grant doesn't explain that. Here's Kate's voice: "I was in a perverse mood, and almost broke, so I took the Metro instead of a taxi."

- Can the writer never explain? Let's not squander our space stating the obvious or explaining what has already been shown. "He put his fist through the wall" doesn't need to be followed with "He was angry." To contemplate, though, to meditate, to interpret, to make connections—these are the writer's charge and duty.

  In Larry Watson's novel *Laura*, the narrator describes the startling contrast between the gloom inside the church during his father's funeral and the beauty of the June day. Watson might have chosen merely to show the contrast and leave it for the reader to infer its meaning, but instead he allowed his narrator to add an explicit comment: "Finally, I believe, over the years in everyone's recollection, death and the day's magnificence knotted and could not be separated. My father's death reminded everyone of how few and precious are such days, and the day in turn put an additional gloss on memories of my father."

  In his remarkable memoir *Goodbye, Darkness*, William Manchester contemplated why so many World War II Marines were capable of ultimate sacrifice and why, thirty-five years after he fought in the South Pacific, he needed to return. "Today their sons wonder why. *I* wonder why. The chasm between generations is one explanation. Perhaps it is the only one. Yet on one level of the subconscious, too deep for me to reach it, I am unsatisfied. So I have nightmares, and so I have returned to the islands to exorcise my inner darkness with the light of understanding."

How can you tell when to let the details alone to make their implications and when to add commentary? If instinct leads you to add explanation, write it in even if you don't know exactly what you're explaining or commenting on. Trust your instinct. At some level, you suspect there's more to the scene than meets the eye. And trust the writing process—the connections, the surprises, what your instinct suspects will be revealed as you go.

Later, scrutinize the explanation. Is it mere platitude? *And that's when I knew that if you truly love something, you must let it go.* Is it simplistic? *War truly is hell.* Does it merely state outright what's already been demonstrated through detail and action? *After the county's distemper epidemic, she made her trailer foster home to thirteen surviving puppies, feeding them warmed formula from an eyedropper every two hours. Clearly, she had a tender heart.*

If any of the above appear in your story, delete them. Nothing lost there. Or ask yourself what your instinct might have been pushing for and why you pulled back in self-protection. Try again until you break through to the connection of the insight you never knew you knew.

But Really—Show, Don't Tell

"The Bug Queen," written by Rachael Cupp back when she was my student, is a simple story. A little girl sits beside her father in church. Nothing much happens. The language is unadorned. And yet by the end we understand a great deal about the child's life. Here is the story to illustrate the power of showing.

> The girl was trying to memorize a part of the sermon when the ladybug landed on her hand. The slight weight surprised her, but she kept herself from moving. Her father was facing the minister, and his face was calm, but she knew better than to trust it. Anything more than the smallest of wiggles would bring his hand down on her arm—a heavy squeeze with a gentle threat of a twist. She looked at him, careful to move only her eyes, and shifted her hands to hide it.
>
> Downstairs the other children were playing. She could hear the muffled sounds of their voices and the occasional wild thumping of someone crashing into a wall. She tried

to shut it out and pay attention to the sermon, knowing she would be tested on it later, but the words sounded slippery. They didn't make any sense. She had never understood why her father thought they were so important.

The ladybug moved in her hand, but it didn't try to escape. She smiled and moved her fingers so she could see it. The minister's voice came a bit louder, and she looked up quickly, but he was still talking about the fires and hell and things. She looked past him and to the window. The sun came through the stained glass, sending blurry patterns of color out onto the altar. The clear pane in the center surrounded the minister with bright spring light.

If he'd say better things it wouldn't be so bad, she thought. It was a pretty place. She liked to look around at the church, pretend it was her house, and not God's. By now, she had memorized every portion of it, knew where she would climb and what windows she would sit in.

If it was my house we could all play the organ, she thought. Her father shifted next to her, and she fastened her eyes forward again. Her side still hurt from earlier, and the pews were shaped strange. It was hard not to move. The ladybug crawled into the hollow between her thumb and first finger, and she had to squash down a giggle at the feel of it.

She looked down at the program, spread out on a hymnal in front of her. It would probably be time for a song soon. Usually she didn't mind, but today they were singing "Onward Christian Soldiers" and she hated that one. She had a nightmare about it once. Everywhere there was burning and blood, and the Christian soldiers were marching through it all. There was a huge cross sort of floating in front of them, with an equally huge Jesus spiked to it. She could see from His face that He was laughing, but the marching drowned out all other sounds.

The girl looked down at the ladybug. It was still moving softly. *When the service is over, I'll get you out of here,* she thought. *This place is no good for anything that's little and alive. Maybe if you go I'll come with you. We'll live forever, somewhere very far away. I'll be the Bug Queen, and when the Christian soldiers come, we'll be ready.*

The congregation rustled around her, and she reached for the hymnal out of habit. Her father unfolded himself from the pew and reached to take a corner of the book. She turned her ladybug hand over quickly, but he saw it. Quickly, without making much sound or changing expression, he grabbed her hand and slammed it forward into the solid wood of the pew in front of them. There was a painful pull in her wrist, and she felt a light, quick warmth across the palm of her hand. The organ began to blare, and her father tapped the page sharply. The warmth had died by the time the first verse started.

This story's success depends on its detail, its language, its playing out of a scene, and its subtext. What if the writer had merely spilled it directly onto the page? *Her father was a harsh, cold, abusive man.* What if she had described the girl's feelings? *She was a scared, lonely, sensitive child.* Instead, the details are precise. Many other details could have been included (stained-glass window colors, other parishioners), but we get the careful, spare selection that suggests the texture of the experience: the other kids playing downstairs, the words of the sermon that sounded slippery, the father unfolding himself.

We know what the child's life is like by what isn't said. In this story, "Her side still hurt from earlier" is more chilling than a depiction of the abuse.

Instead of summary, we see the scene. The child has been through this before: She knows she'll be quizzed on the sermon; she knows if she wiggles, her father will twist her arm. But this time something is different. It's only a ladybug, moving "softly," but this time in the father's cold violence (look at those verbs—"grabbed," "slammed"), the little girl loses her hope of escape.

With this little story, Rachael Cupp learned some early essential lessons about writing: "It represents my first really successful story, the first time I set out to write a certain story, in a certain voice, and was able to accomplish it. For a writer, that's huge: so often we go into a piece with grand expectations that we fail to fulfill entirely. Additionally, the story represents many features that are early representations of my writing style: simple and specific details, third-person limited point of view, and brevity. . . . I went on to make it into a short film, and to include it in various discussions of writing and the evolution of style over time. For such a short piece, it's done a lot of heavy lifting in my writing life."

Look at your story. Where does suggestive detail convey the power of the experience? Leave it be. Anything added will only lessen it. Where can you connect an experience years ago to a recent trouble? Or where can you contemplate the nuances of a complicated experience? Or where can you extrapolate comments about the complexities of the human condition from your individual experience? Write it in. And later scrutinize it when it's cooled off. Does it state the obvious or go somewhere new? Write it in. You can always write it out. That's what erasers and the delete key are for.

Begin your own heavy lifting by keeping it light: by careful selection of detail, by scene creation, by omission of explanations, by trust in the power of subtext to evoke the story's emotional and psychological truths.

The Truth About Details

The details in scenes and the ways those details are described depend on who is telling the story. The purpose of descriptions and metaphors is not admirable writing. They exist to bring scenes to life, yes—but at the same time to reveal who is doing the seeing and that narrator's state of mind and heart.

Prove it to yourself. First, picture your bathroom. Second, imagine yourself a woman in that bathroom who has just taken a home pregnancy test. It's positive. Third, write five different two-sentence descriptions of the bathroom, each one to match a different reaction to the news: (1) shock, (2) anger, (3) joy, (4) fear, (5) relief.

How did the selection of details differ among descriptions? How did the ways details were described differ? How did the details and descriptions work to show or suggest the feelings?

In Daniel Orozco's story "Hunger Tales," a father and son have just returned from the funeral of the wife/mother. It is the day before Thanksgiving, and the mortician gives them a box containing an entire prepared turkey dinner. In their loss, they aren't really hungry but pretty soon they're wolfing down everything. "They peeled off strips of meat with their fingers and dipped them into the gravy. They spooned sauce and yams and mashed potatoes. They sopped up turkey grease from their plates with hunks of bread. They discovered a mother lode of stuffing within the turkey's cavity." Orozco never tells us about the emptiness they're trying to stuff, their neediness for the sustenance they've lost, the comfort they're trying to stock up on against the loss to come. We know.

In Richard Yates' novel *Disturbing the Peace*, an alcoholic having a breakdown is at a very fancy restaurant. The New York Strip Sirloins "turned out to be the heaviest slabs of meat he had ever seen. He looked fixedly at his portion and knew that if only he could cut into it and eat it some balance might be restored to the evening . . . but the sight of it was nauseating. So was the sight of his huge baked potato, its own bulk overwhelmed by a gout of sour cream and chives, and so was the glistening amplitude of his salad." The words describing the food ("slabs," "bulk," "gout," "glistening amplitude") reveal the man's state, and we know this dinner is not going to end well.

Show Yourself

It is Thanksgiving. The family is gathered for the feast. Something bad has happened to one person at the table.

Write a scene from that person's perspective *without mentioning the bad thing*. What is on the table? Who is present? What do the people say? What do they do?

Tomorrow, revisit your scene. Highlight the specific details that capture the atmosphere, that suggest the texture of this family gathering. Underline the phrases that indirectly reveal relationships and feelings.

Cross out lines that explain.

Reconsider any details that work against the scene's undercurrents, that mislead. Cross them out or alter them.

Now revise the scene, omitting the crossed-out parts.

Read it aloud. Admire the invisible currents shimmering above the page and running beneath it.

Saying the Unsayable

Spelling things out is safe. Stating the obvious is easy. But offering pat explanations is belittling and disrespectful to all players involved, the writer included.

Writing the truth is risky. It means facing the lurid details, the unvarnished details, the bluntly graphic details. But the experience's hold on you, the reason you're compelled to write about it, deserves the whole truth, without escape into easy explanation.

Your strong writing will say what can't quite be put into words. Your words will be specific, you will name names, your language will be sharp and honed. Your commentary and contemplations will take readers where they (and you) couldn't have arrived at alone. And between the crisp lines and all that is left implied or silent is the truth that is unsayable.

The risk in the writing and the honesty in the rewriting are worth it. I'd say more but I'd be violating my own advice.

5

TELLING IT SLANT:
USING INDIRECTION TO REVEAL TRUTH

As a child, I hid in our big house's rec room in the basement and wrote my secrets into a lockable book. The studio couch was beside the laundry chute opening. In junior high, my sisters and I listened from the upstairs bathroom to our parents' New Year's Eve party and took turns looking down the chute, catching glimpses of a woman's hands crossing over her knees as she danced the Charleston or of hands holding out a cup to be filled with red punch. Over the music we caught snatches of talk ("Lela said she just could never . . ." "Will you look at Larry") and then later the giggles and moans that accompanied a game somehow involving a sheet; then, later still, someone at the old upright piano and the women's and men's voices together singing "Auld Lang Syne," and over it, the tugging sweetness of our mother's voice singing descant.

When I was a high school senior, my baby sophomore sisters listened and peeked down that laundry chute when I played pool with my boyfriend (hey, I wasn't *that* shy) and when we made out on the brown couch. To embarrass me, they threw underwear down the chute.

How much of this is true?

The house was big. However, a recent trip to my home town revealed the magnifying effects of adolescence and memory. Some years ago I found my old diaries, and they did have locks (pickable with a paper clip) so that part's true. I might have just invented the paper clip, though. I know I made up snatches of dialogue, though a Lela and a Larry would have been present. I know my mother showed us the Charleston in the living room. I don't really know if they danced it at the party. More likely they were trying to jitterbug.

I suspect it was years later that my mother described the game: Behind the curtain of a sheet, all the men took off their pants and in the dark, each woman tried to identify her particular husband's knees and calves by feel. Certainly there must have been giggles and moans. Right?

I'm certain there was, for a while, a jangly upright piano in the rec room (did it precede or coexist with my upstairs baby grand?), but probably I made up the singing, though my mother could do a lovely harmony. In truth, I remember myself spying on my cousin making out downstairs, but my sisters swear they dropped the underwear down on *my* make-out session.

I asked my sisters if they could recall memories of the New Year's Eve party.

Susan: "Well, I remember more about spying on *you* through the laundry chute than spying on Mom and Dad. I vaguely remember the New Year's Eve party and have fleeting thoughts of music, party clothes, lots of noise (mainly drunken laughter), and groping hands. We glimpsed Mom dancing with another man and were shocked."

Sally: "I remember shooting underpants down on you while you entertained old what's-his-name. But I don't remember a great deal about spying on the New Year's Eve party other than my shock at seeing seeing Dad with Lela, or perhaps Lizzie Rae, on his lap. I think he was drunk. Everyone was kissing and not their spouses. We knew what they were doing was naughty and somehow dangerous."

Susan and Sally are identical twins and were spying witnesses to the same party, but one remembers the mother and the other the father. And they say they don't remember much!

What's a writer to do? We're digging in the trash heap of memory for truth and all we're finding is lots of interesting junk. How do we know if we're unearthing the shards of other people's history, read or heard about or imagined, or a broken tricycle that certainly *looks* a lot like ours, but did it have those plastic streamers on the handlebars? How do we know the exact year of the stratum of artifact we've reached?

Do Facts Matter?

Sometimes they don't matter. My laundry chute memories, factually accurate or not, offer a better sense of my childhood and family than facts I know or could check. I was born in . . . my father worked at . . . we moved to . . . the public record lists the facts, but the private record, however inaccurate or unverifiable, reveals another sort of truth.

And the light of memory shifts, so that depending on the season of viewing, some events are spotlit and some details are in shadow. Right now, I'm feeling fond of the laundry chute and the secure childhood it returned to me. (I'm trying to ignore my sisters' memories and those fears aroused in children when they brush up against the mysteries of the alien adult world.)

But when I was working on my novel *The Third Law of Motion*, other memories of the laundry chute came to light. I wrote about my character Dulcie's eavesdropping on her parents arguing in the basement. I wrote about her (okay, my) ritual of dropping clothes down the laundry chute one item at a time, each accompanied by one word of a chant: Look-out-Kitty-Willow-if-you're-down-there. We had a gray kitten, and I was afraid the falling clothes would smother her. It was only in writing about the ritual that I remembered the rest of the chant—which-I-know-you-aren't—and knew what I'd forgotten: that Willow, whose birth in the hamper I had watched (ecstatic and terrified), had died. Everything was out of control. That was a different laundry chute altogether.

Which childhood portrait is true?

If we're looking for factual truth, I could travel back to Michigan and knock again on the door of the house on Homecrest Avenue and explain my quest. The people who live there would let me in (if you say you're a writer, people will tell you and show you just about anything), and I'd climb the bannistered stairs (do they still have a bannister? did they ever?) to the upstairs bathroom and determine whether a child standing on the toilet seat could in fact peer down the laundry chute. Other details and events could be researched.

But facts don't always matter. When you're capturing the flavor of a place and time, the quality and texture of an experience, revealing details are worth more than any historical record. The details that show up when you write may not match those of any of the other players in the drama, but they are your truth. You may accidentally or deliberately conflate details and incidents from different times, but the new picture they make is a deeper truth than historically accurate snapshots. When it's emotional truth you seek, trust memory's details to find it. Memory, as you are writing, will decide the quality of light shined on the details.

What light is shed on memory's details depends on the position of the rememberer. When I first made notes about the kitten, my mother had cancer. I was angry and in denial. She has been dead now for years, and I am still purely missing her. I just want to hear her descant rising above the living voices. The details you recall and what they suggest about the meaning of the experience change depending on where you are—literally in terms of distance from events but also emotionally and psychologically in terms of your life in the meanwhile.

Sometimes facts sort of matter.

An inaccurate detail can make readers begin to question other details rather than trust the writer. In a novel by a respected writer, the characters live in New York City, where I've only played tourist. Everything seemed accurate, and I believed the details and the places. Later, the character takes a road trip west and in downtown Phoenix swerves to avoid hitting a dead armadillo. I've done time in Phoenix and I've gotta tell you, there are no armadillos there, alive or dead. I tried to help out the writer—well, maybe it fell off a truck just up from Texas?—but it was hard work. I stopped believing the story.

In nonfiction, too, inaccuracies call other aspects of the story into question. *No, Dickie, Jr., wasn't even born until 1986, so there's no way you could have been baby-sitting him in the summer of 1984 when you were changing his diaper and he peed straight up into your face. I bet you made that up, too. How can I take your word for any of this?*

Sometimes facts really matter. If Dickie, Jr., is ready to sue, you can remind him that the defense against libel is truth. This time we're talking factual truth.

Nancy E. Turner, author of many historical novels, points out that "asserting 'this novel is a work of fiction: any similarity with any real person living or dead is purely coincidental' will not save you if the idiot/loser/maniac you've characterized is easily recognized from the brilliantly accurate description. As for nonfiction: If your work causes the damaged parties "to lose their job, family, or costs them any other way, you may be liable for damages. The term 'punitive damages' refers to humiliation, embarrassment, stress, mental anguish, and always involves cash."

Journalist Roy Peter Clark, writing about the line between fact and fiction, describes for nonfiction writers "two cornerstone principles: Do not add. Do not deceive."

The solution? In fiction, alter the details. In nonfiction, get the facts straight. If they're correct, you're protected against libel. And you have every right to your opinions.

Or write a poem. I've never heard of a poet being sued for libel.

Telling It Slant

In my sister Susan's email about the party memories, she added: "The thing that makes the laundry chute images so enticing was that they were just quick glimpses and bits of conversation that left lots to the imagination."

That's what memory does, too.

That's what the story on the page does, too.

Instead of painting a panorama, the storyteller zeros in. Focus on this. Instead of describing the scene fully and directly, the storyteller gives us glimpses, and what is seen in those glimpses totally depends on who is doing the glimpsing. Susan saw Mom. Sally saw Dad.

Emily Dickinson knew the way: "Tell all the Truth but tell it slant."

The way into the story is through the laundry chute. (All right, the chute went straight down and we're talking slant, but stay with me here. This is a metaphor.)

In art, we are never quite shown the full picture. Imagine a Japanese sumi-e painting of a bamboo branch and leaves. We need only a few black ink brush strokes to know what we are seeing. In the sketchiness, we *see* the bamboo more acutely that we would in a photograph or picture in a guide to trees. It's true that sometimes less is more. What my sisters and I saw isolated in the square of the laundry chute's opening was more powerful than the full-blown party scene would have been, I'm pretty sure. (Now I'm sorry we didn't just go downstairs in our jammies and teach them how to do the twist. You know they wanted to.)

Similarly, the writer selects details, omits, and exaggerates to reveal not facts but the real truth. In Picasso's *Guernica*, a gigantic mural painted after Nazi planes bombed the Spanish town of Guernica in 1937, the face of an open-mouthed woman and her outstretched arm holding a light emerge from a window, beholding a stark, twisted, surreal scene of pointed-tongued animals and distorted, wailing humans. The angles and distortions suggest the horror of war as no direct account could. Picasso himself said, "The artist lies in order to tell the truth."

Slant is at an angle. Slant is sideways, not head on. Slant is under the table, not above board. Slant will blindside you.

If I'd asked my sisters for their feelings about our childhood, I'd have heard, I imagine, that we went to Lake Michigan in the summer, we lived in a big white house, we loved our parents, they loved us. True enough, but limited. And superficial. Instead, when they came at the memories sideways, they talked about shock and danger, with the unspoken complexities of children's interpretations of adult behavior and nervous fears running beneath.

Why should we tell our truths slant? Here's Dickinson's answer: "The Truth must dazzle gradually/Or every man be blind."

What Dickinson knew in 1868 is still a significant lesson for writers today. The poem's first line makes her point affirming that, indeed, you should write *all* the truth but that the way to tell it is "slant." And why is that? Why should you take a roundabout journey to truth? The power of your Truth (maybe we should keep Dickinson's capital T) is, head-on, too intense. Truth shined directly into our eyes would blind us.

For yourself in your search and for your readers, coming at Truth indirectly is the way to illuminate it.

What I Did on My Summer Vacation

One of the problems with telling a story straight is a tedious recitation of facts and events, an endless (to the audience) travelogue, slide or video show with full commentary. *We did, we saw, we climbed, we ate.* In the tedium, nobody else gets to go along for the ride. (I'm sorry to sound cross, but spare me the photos of your plates at restaurants.)

Telling it straight, with a rigid filling in of the facts, can lead to a series of anecdotes. This happened, that happened, and this happened. With an anecdote, we're waiting for the rest that never comes. *Yes? And your point is . . . ?* But a story shapes the material so we come to know the reason we've been following along. (Sometimes the writer has figured out the reason only two steps ahead of the reader. Okay, I say.)

A story—in fiction, in nonfiction, and in poetry—has a plot. Narrative writing has a story line. A random series of events—this happened and later this happened, just one damned thing after another—is mere anecdote. Plot depends on cause and effect. This happened because that happened. Plots depend on connections. *Oh! The little ritual of the laundry chute chant was an attempt to control things that were frightening and mysterious to a little girl: parents fighting, the quick path of birth to death.* And it is the writer's job to sit at the desk and set down the memories in detail, in scene, until the plot shows itself.

And so She Told Him ...

I've been urging you simultaneously to make full-frontal confrontation with the truth and yet to approach it sideways or from the rear. Why? A full-frontal approach, especially when it's about other people, is gossip. Or when it's about the writer, it's self-pity or self-promotion, however honest and humble the intentions. It may appear to have a plot—*and that's how I learned . . .*—but it remains superficial.

The writer's purpose has a great deal to do with the story that emerges. Writing a tell-all (for money, why else?) smacks to me of exploitation. *Pssst. I have the dirt on someone famous. Wanna see?* Whistleblowers are good, but tattletales . . . every kid knows the view of tattletales and knows the difference. And I'm not just saying this because I don't know the secrets of anyone famous. I do.

Writing to help others is certainly more noble a purpose. I appreci-ate—I honor—the desire to help others negotiate and survive the rough path, but (you heard that "but" coming) that purpose is inherently lim-iting. Often it's premature, for the writer doesn't know the connections and the insights until they have shown themselves in the writing itself. Sometimes, even while it's passionate, it's didactic: *I know now . . . so you should . . .* The zealot writes propaganda, and thus has actually a lesser chance of influencing those who have been set on the path of grief and pain than the writer who simply tells the moving story.

This is why I favor narrative over lyric writing: that is, storytelling that uses scenes and characters to get at truth slantwise as opposed to more direct expressions of feelings or beliefs. Certainly fine lyric writ-ing has its methods of indirection (see Lia Purpura's powerful lyric essay "Autopsy Report") but too often it just rips its heart out and sets it on a platter.

Writers seek to explore and discover rather than to express them-selves or communicate. I don't want the writer to *share* with me. It's egotistical and intrusive. I mean, in person, how can you say no when your neighbor says, "May I share with you my feelings about when my kitty died?" That's the beauty of "share": The listener can't say no with-out coming across as a heartless jerk. Of course, that's why this conno-tation of "share" was invented. It's a command: You must listen to me; you're a heartless jerk if you don't. Readers don't want to be bullied.

Write first for yourself. Remember, you don't know the answers until you have written them. Let the writing serve its true purpose: to lead you to your truths. They will affect and help others more, much more, than lesson plans.

No Cheese, Please

In the beginning, writers may be pleased when their writings are labe-led "sentimental." After all, they *wanted* lots of feeling. Then they learn the definition of sentimentality: writing that is smarmy, gooey, cheesy, schmaltzy, and sappy. (That's a little literary lingo for you.) For example:

> He looked at me with dancing azure eyes. The silence was deafening. When at last he uttered the words I'd been cry-ing and dying to hear—"I love you more than life itself, my darling"—my soul swooned. It was the happiest moment of my life.

Hand me a barf bag.

Certainly we want feeling and sentiment in our writing, but we can't tell readers what to feel: We can only set down the details and scenes of our experiences, and hope. Writer Carol Emshwiller advised: "Don't do all the crying for the reader." You may shed some tears onto your pages, but tearstains alone won't make your readers cry. You must let them witness or live through your story rather than merely hear how it made you feel. Then they'll read it and weep.

From a Distance

Trying to write *Meridian 144* on Guam, I couldn't see the jungle for the banyans. I looked out the window above my desk at the flap-ping banana tree leaves, at the snake twisting down an ironwood trunk and beyond to the ocean's blues advancing to the horizon, from light and shallow to deep Prussian. When I wrote about the reality before my eyes, the descriptions might have been suitable for a natu-ralist's guide or a tourist brochure, but not the true picture I wanted to reveal.

Many find it works better to write about a place after they've left it. The mind's eye sees the true details.

This suggestion applies not only to place but also to experience. Occasionally a writer in the midst of turmoil can capture the incan-descence for the page, especially perhaps in poems. It's worth trying, if only to record details for later use, if only for therapeutic value. Usually, though, we find our experiences' truths when we look backward, when we squint, when we see from afar.

Writing Slant

Often when beginning artists draw an object they are looking at, such as a chair, the results are awkward and labored. With the chair right in front of them, they are stuck in the literal, the factual. In an intriguing method of teaching drawing called "flash lab," developed by Hoyt Sherman, the beginning artists sit before their sketchpads and then the lights are turned off. An image, such as a chair, is projected onto a screen for a tenth of a second. Then, still in the dark, the artists draw the afterimage of the flash. The results are fresh, lively, and original as they catch the essence of the chair. The beginners produce drawings much beyond their level of skill and experience.

Often the image projected was turned upside down, so that the "thingness" of the object was missing from the students' renderings. They were merely responding to afterimages from the neck down, so to speak. Often when they "recognized" the object from the afterimage, they were sorely disappointed because the recognition interfered with the quality of their work.

Here's a writing experiment to try. Sit before your computer, fingers in position. Close your eyes. Think of the house you grew up in. Wander from room to room until you come to one you'd rather not enter. Go inside anyway. In your mind's eye, picture this room. Still with your eyes closed, without thinking, type words and phrases to describe what you "see." What details show up? What experience happened in the room?

Don't stop to correct anything. Let the associations flow from your mind's eye through your hands.

Here's an example:

> Upstairs bathroom laundry chute end of studio couch right below me as a teenager staring down at my cousin she's making out with her boyfriend their heads right below the opening her on the bottom all of a sudden her eyes open and she stares right up at me two floors above her face to face I catch her in intimacy, I am part of it now, and she has been caught she is guilty and I am guilty and yet I am so far away and I wonder about their bodies that I can't see pictures from my friend Pat's brother's dirty book the impossibility of the sketches of men and women stuck together I back away from the laundry chute and close its door silently did my cousin, seen and unseen, continue kissing her boyfriend? The house is full of quickened breath

Later these notes helped me capture the intensity and mystery of adolescent sexuality in *The Third Law of Motion*.

In your darkness, afterimages remain. They may be less coherent than my sample. Good, I say. Type them however they appear. Stay in the dark until your hands begin to "see" what happened in the room and what it meant.

Then with open eyes, print out what your closed eyes saw. Now write the scene or poem embedded in the flashes of memory of the page. Leave the edges rough and the shapes distorted.

The Ladder of Tears

My student Alan Brich wrote a crossbred story/poem that captures memory's afterimages. Here are the first sections of "The Ladder of Tears."

Some Days

I'm building a ladder of tears.

It has twelve rungs so far.   It's not finished.

Close but not yet.

It takes thirty-five tears

to make a strong rung. Thirty tears make a rung

but I wouldn't feel safe.

without the extra five for support.

I spend my days collecting tears

to build a ladder.

I have a bowl under my bed

I put the tears in it while I'm waiting

to gather enough to make a rung.

I usually find ten or so tears a day.

Some days are better than others.

I found twenty-three today.

Fourteen before noon.

Quite a day for finding tears.

No Coffee-Morning Walk

This is how it starts:

        I wake up this morning

        go to make some coffee.   I like coffee

                          I'm out of filters.

            No coffee.

I have some money

so I get dressed and go out to find some.

            I start walking

                  toward a diner

          a couple blocks south of where I live.

        It's early.

        The air is still cold from the night before.

It pulls the skin tight on my face.

The cars are starting to wake

        from their garage slumber.   They drive the sleep

                out of their headlights.

I walk about a block and

        already smell breakfast rising

            from the diner

                like a fat butter sun.

A Wallet With a Snap

        I make it to the parking lot of the diner.

            Some letters have fallen off the sign.

            Maybe they ran off and

           joined another word somewhere.

The sign says   "Ed's Rest nt

Just like Mom's."

That's where I find the first tear.

It's sitting right under

the word "Mom" on the sign

like a forgotten dewdrop.

I knew right then

it was going to be a good day for collecting tears.

I pick up the tear

and put it in my wallet.

I have a special pocket in my wallet

where I put the tears that I find.

It has a snap.

Most people would probably put nickels

or dimes in it.   Not me.

I put tears in it.

I put nickels and dimes in the front pocket of my jeans

when I have nickels and dimes

to put anywhere.

Brich seems to have invented just the right form for this story, which goes on to recount more tear-gatherings, how the ladder is built, and finally the purpose of the ladder. The straightforward, sometimes flat statements take on extra import and significance when arranged as lines. The line breaks and spaces provide neat surprises. The unusual structure suits the strangeness of the story's concept (collecting tears? saving them in a wallet? building a ladder out of them? oh, really?).

In addition to the form, other elements helped Brich tell this story slant: the carefully chosen specific details ("Ed's Rest nt/Just like Mom's"), the figurative language (the cars that "drive the sleep/out of their headlights"), the off-kilter view (the fallen letters that might have run off and "joined another word somewhere"), the omissions (what clothes the narrator is wearing, for instance, or what else is in his wallet), the exaggerations and distortions (the very notion of making a ladder out of tears, the number of tears required to make a rung), and the straightforward presentation of the fantastical concept, without explanations. The story comes at the meaning of tears indirectly.

Like the character in Brich's story who must build the ladder to understand its purpose, a writer builds a story by gathering memories and designing a bowl to hold them until truth climbs up into brightness.

Can You Hear Me Now?

Why do we ask questions? Occasionally we're actually seeking information. Politicians ask questions to dismiss uncomfortable situations and get on with what they really want to say. "Were mistakes made? Yes. But . . ." "Do I wish I'd done things differently? Absolutely. But . . ." Sometimes we truly want answers from our family and friends.

Often we ask a question for the same reason I did here: so we can proceed to say what we want to say.

Another slantwise way of approaching strong material, political or personal, is by asking questions rather than making statements. See Wendell Berry's devastating poem "Questionnaire." See Laura Van Etten's disturbing and ultimately affirming story "Questions Before We Start," published in *Ninth Letter*. Posing questions rather than providing direct answers is also a slantwise way of exploring material from different angles, looking at it every which way, as in Stephen Dunn's poem "If a Clown."

My student Danyelle Khmara, looking for a way to deal with a significant relationship concern in her life, tried simply asking questions:

Would You Call This Home If

Would you call this home if

it had a pink bathtub,

a rotary phone, and

an aluminum ashtray

from the 70's? Would you

stay if the piano was here—

the old upright

that brought you

to tears when you didn't know

if or how? Would you

call this yours if

the colorful jars that the two

of you found and carefully

washed of their desert solitude

were on display? If you saw

your old sewing machine

with the gold inlays, placed

in just the right spot—

then would you

say home? Would you

know you were home if

you slept tangled

into each other as often

as back to back? Would you

be able to call it home

without obtaining a guarantee,

acknowledging the failure rate,

having heard the statistics? If

you put pictures of children

on the fridge? Listened

to the songs he played when

you first met? Only wore the perfume

that took both of you back—

then, would you be daring

enough to call this home?

Could you fall asleep naked

and not wake till

the morning? Could you

spend your savings and abandon

social media? Could you

look at the varicose veins

without cringing? Could you

forgive yourself for

not doing it right, for

getting older, for all the times

you were mean? If you

chose to believe

that you are

loved, regardless

of your most brutal

mistake or your brightest

triumph, then

would you call this home?

Listing items her partner saved from a landfill and had come to cherish, mixed in with her own treasures, Khmara realized what the question was: "Could I ever be brave enough (or foolish enough) to combine my things and my life with his? Interwoven are my greatest fears and deepest longings." Did asking the series of poignant questions lead her to a conclusion? What do you think?

Practicing Slant

1. Pick a time when you were especially confused about events or people in your life. Remember the house or apartment where you lived at that time. Focus on one room that normally saw interaction and activity—the living room, kitchen, or family room. Imagine a chute down into that room. (Forget logic. Of course, laundry shouldn't drop onto the kitchen table. Of course, a chute shouldn't originate on the roof.) Now peer down the chute. You aren't present down in the room, merely observing from above. In your single square of the view below, what do you see? What do you make of it?

2. Remember or imagine an open coffin holding a body. Now without mentioning the coffin or the body, write a detailed description of what surrounds it.

3. Think of a person or character (other than yourself) who's an important part of your story. Stand that person up, turn out the light, and, flashlight in hand, walk around behind that person. Write a description of your person from the rear (and not just *the* rear).

4. Hold your pencil above column A below. Close your eyes and zap the pencil down on one of the words. Circle it. Repeat with column B.

A	B
rowboat	feathers
doghouse	teeth
refrigerator	toenails
cape	flames
rope	bones
mannequin	fins
shield	shadows
bridge	alphabet letters

Write a set of specific instructions for constructing your A word from your B word. How to build a rowboat out of bones, for instance. You may acknowledge the difficulty of this strange task but not the impossibility.

5. Write a poem or memoir fragment or short-short story using all (or mostly) questions. Include specific details. Just ask, without answering.

The laundry-chute focus frames and isolates pieces of the picture rather than delineating the whole picture. The mysterious fragments reveal greater truth than any fully described and explained scene.

In painting, negative space frames an object and positions it. In music, we hear the spaces between the notes as well as the notes themselves. The coffin-avoidance exercise shows how you can suggest the truth of an object or event by looking not at it but at what surrounds it.

Another way to startle the truth into revealing itself is by looking at the story's people or events from another angle, as in the third exercise. The normal face-to-face view often shows pretty much what we expect to see, while an unusual angle or lighting may show us the surprises.

These exercises will give you special practice in methods of indirection that you can apply to telling your stories slant.

The willingness to be nonlinear, playful, even nonsensical catches the spirit of slant. So go all the way, into the ridiculous, the distorted, the fantastic, to know what that spirit feels like. Whether or not your stories venture into fantasyland, take that spirit along for your great ride.

Our truths are sly. They want to keep their secrets. Apply the tricks of coming at them slantwise and they'll show themselves.

Our truths also want to be known. Tell them slant and their power will not blind but will illuminate you and your readers.

6

CHOOSING DIRECTIONS:
CONSIDERING GENRE CHOICES

Do you swear to tell the truth, the whole truth, and nothing but the truth?

Think carefully here. Your answers will guide your choice of genre. Should you tell your story in fiction? Personal essay or memoir? Poem? How can you choose?

Put Yourself on the Stand

Tell yourself the truth. With your story material in mind, write out answers to these questions (without thinking of the implications of those answers):

1. Why do you want to tell this story? What is your purpose in writing it?
2. How certain can you be of the actual facts of the story?
3. What voices could tell the story?
4. Who might be harmed by exposure of the actual facts?

Poetry or Prose?

Usually there's no question. You're a writer whose proclivities naturally run one way or the other. Or the story itself selects its form, and the decision is out of your hands.

Many writers, though, are naturally responsive to various genres, and some writers' genres of choice aren't really their natural proclivity. How can you tell? Try asking these questions: What do you write without waiting for inspiration? What do you read? I, for one, write articles, personal essays, poems, and fiction. The nonfiction results from an assignment. The poetry waits for inspiration. As you may have guessed, it's fiction that I work regularly on, responding to *its* command and need, not my own or any editor's. And though I read poetry, nonfiction, and short story collections, the majority of the books on my "keep" shelf and the books I most eagerly check out of the library are novels. No matter what I once thought I was, no matter what I most want to be, my heart is a blazing novelist's.

At any rate, whether a particular story should be poetry or prose (fiction or nonfiction) depends more on the writer's purpose and on the material's requirements than on what form the writer usually practices.

Writer Margaret Atwood said that when she and her brother were children, they liked to pick up rocks to see what worms, insects, and reptiles were underneath. Sometimes they'd just look, and sometimes they'd poke the critters with a stick. For Atwood, a poem picks up the rock and contemplates the material, but fiction pokes it with a stick to see what happens. If your purpose is to reflect on the nuanced, complex, or startling meaning of the story's events, then poetry may be the way to go. If your purpose is to show a complicated series of events that shaped a life, prose is more likely to serve.

If you can't decide, don't even try to. Simply approach the story in whatever form feels better for you or for the material. You should usually trust your instinct. But if, in the writing, you find out the choice wasn't really right, then you can direct the story to a different evolutionary path.

Years ago, writer Sherryl Clark wrote a poem to capture emotion for herself, through images:

> Choosing What to Keep
>
>
> On hot sticky vinyl
>
> in the back seat of the old Austin
>
> I squirm, deliberating this enormous question:
>
> Are you coming in to see your mother?
>
> I am small, a child
>
> dressed in starched cotton and lace
>
> and the funeral home
>
> looms spectre-like.
>
> The day hangs on my answer

promising big person status

if I agree.

Mum is: knitting at the football,

soft curling hair under my brush,

apple slice for tennis,

her blue pleated dress

swinging around her knees.

Not staring eyes and sunken cheeks,

a memory to twist and blur the others.

For just a little longer

I choose to stay small.

Just as the child in the poem chooses the images that keep her mother alive for her, the poem itself preserves, through those private images, the heartbreaking time of self-protected innocence. Clark said that she turned to poetry first because it allowed her to stick with the images and look at the experience sideways rather than confront it head on.

Later, returning to the material, she wanted to tell more of the story and explore just who she was in a way that created a fuller picture. As she wrote "With These Hands," the process of writing the essay, just for herself without considering publication, called up more and more details.

Here is the opening:

When my mother laughs, her laughter is like smooth round pebbles falling through clear water. She sits in the dark passageway of our ancient house, Bakelite telephone to her ear and listens to careful secrets spilling from its heart. We cannot hear what she is talking about, but the secrets swirl down the passageway like smoke, patterning the cool air and sliding into the tattered books crammed onto the shelves near the bathroom.

She has been baking cakes today and they cool on the wooden table, stacked on wire racks, waiting to be stowed in round tins that fit under the cupboards. One tin is Wedgewood blue with a white lace trim, another holds a faded photograph of a slim queen in blue on a horse that strolls across a cobbled courtyard. The tins echo when they're empty; they clang together as if demanding sustenance, like children who clamour for cake, more cake.

Usually there is a tray of apple or apricot slice dusted with white, cloudy sugar, sometimes a chocolate cake, plain because icing is a luxury, and always a mountainous pile of biscuits—golden crisp Anzacs, gingernuts as hard as toffee that have to be dunked, cinnamon crisps that crumble and melt. She fills the echoing tins and closes their lids with a firm and satisfied hand, and the smell of glistened sugar and golden syrup lingers in the air all afternoon.

The cakes are for my father, who wakes before dawn to herd sleepy cows into the concrete yards where they're milked by machines that slurp and suck creamy streams through shining steel pipes. My mother also milks cows, bending to tie leg ropes and ducking sly kicks from cows still grumpy from being woken. Later she fills buckets with warm milk and feeds the calves in the paddock, soothing their loneliness with mother's food and allowing them to avidly suck her fingers as they search for the answer to un-nameable need. Once a calf sucked her wedding ring off her finger and swallowed it, gulping and drinking and wandering away to play with the others. For days we walked around the paddock with long sticks, sifting through brown calf dung, hoping to see a flash of gold, but to no avail. Her hands remain bare—her square diamond-chip engagement ring has long since worn through, its slim encirclement thinning to nothingness.

In the essay, the reader learns the details and significance of the poem's images, the knitting, the apple slice, the blue pleated dress, drawing the full portrait of the mother and revealing the author's New Zealand childhood and, at the end, poignantly acknowledging the innocence now lost:

> At home my mother is working in the kitchen, cleaning
> and tidying, possibly cooking lunch or preparing food with
> her deft hands, when she feels faint and her heart pounds
> with an agonizing beat. She grips the wooden bench,
> drops the spoon she is holding and lowers herself onto the
> floor, trying to catch her breath, waiting for the pain to ease
> a little. She leans back against the small wooden cupboard
> where the special cups and dishes are kept, lowers her
> hand and dies, alone.
>
> I continue to hit tennis balls and eat apple slice, my father
> fetches meat from the butchers, the cows stand outside
> the fenced garden, and, in the store room, row upon row
> of coloured jars stand in silent order.

Sherryl Clark says she couldn't have written the essay at the time she wrote the poem. She kept the poem spare and contained. Later, she told herself she would "just go for it" in the essay, now offering the details to evoke and explore the losses and the love.

Read the complete essay here: http://sherrylclark.com/WithTheseHands.htm.

How can you tell if the story wants to be poem or prose? You can't, not always. Try the poem, and see what happens. If more details than the infrastructure of a poem can support keep adding their weight, if other people in the story insist on showing up, use the poem as the warm-up and then bring the star act onto the stage and write the full scenes in prose. If the poem dissatisfies you and feels too easy, forced into poetry's box, then approach the story as prose, with its elbow room.

If you need to poke the story with a stick to prod it into action, write the prose. But if you can look closely at the story and come to understand, write the poem. If the sharp and allusive details lead to interpretation of their meaning, then trust poetry's ultimate power.

And then sometimes it's just a matter of timing, what we are ready to know.

Fiction and Nonfiction: The Three Differences

It's not always simple to separate stories into the distinct categories of fiction and nonfiction. We have the "nonfiction novel," we have novels featuring characters who share authors' names, we have college students who refer to any book or play as a novel, and we have memoirs that turn out to be fabrications. When Andrew Cozine sent "Hand Jive" to *The Iowa Review*, editors assumed it was fiction and it was soon selected for *The Best American Short Stories 1995*. However, the autobiographical story was written for a nonfiction class at Columbia University. One of my favorite memoirs, *This Boy's Life*, has the feel of a novel, but in the opening, author Tobias Wolff tells us: "I have been corrected on some points, mostly of chronology. Also my mother thinks that a dog I describe as ugly was actually quite handsome. I've allowed some of these points to stand, because this is a book of memory, and memory has its own story to tell. But I have done my best to make it a truthful story."

Despite the blurring, three major differences keep fiction and nonfiction stories in separate categories.

The Truth

First, nonfiction is bound to factual truth, while unbound fiction can play fast and loose with details of the actual experience. On the witness stand, "truth" equals facts. If you tell your story as nonfiction (personal essay, memoir), you won't necessarily tell "the whole truth" (unless you mean to write a ten-volume history), but you are promising to tell "nothing but the truth." Certainly nonfiction borrows techniques from fiction and some license is allowed, for example to re-create dialogue that nobody conveniently recorded, but nonfiction writers promise to tell the factual truth, as much as they can know it, and to interpret it honestly. Readers have the right to trust the implicit promise.

Voice

The second difference between fiction and nonfiction is voice. Who is telling the story? In nonfiction, the voice belongs to the writer. In fiction, the voice belongs to a character. I'm oversimplifying here, but the distinction is significant. Any story needs a strong voice telling it. It is the power of a compelling voice whispering its secrets or insisting on its views or hollering its truths that conveys the story. But how much can readers trust the voice? How reliable is it? Nonfiction promises an honest voice exploring the owner's experiences. Nonfiction's voice is Diogenes relinquishing conventional wisdom, sleeping in a bare honest tub, scrutinizing the facts of experience in search of truth. Fiction's voice is not so trustworthy. In its search for truth, fiction's light is held not aloft but tilted. Fiction's voices are sneaky or defensive, slippery or cocky. In their exaggeration, they insist on being heard: Listen to *my* truth. They can't quite be taken at face value. They report the world as seen from their subjective angle of vision. Reading fiction, we have to bend down or twist around or stand on our heads to see things as the unreliable storyteller does, and then we have to interpret them. Fiction's voice comes at truth sideways.

Structure

Third, fiction is made up of scenes that show relationships, events, connections, and emotion, but nonfiction gets to play show *and* tell. Fiction goes to third grade and holds up before the class a vivid, colorful, carefully painted picture, and says, "Here it is, make of it what you will." Nonfiction props the picture up before the other boys and girls, picks up a laser pointer, takes the mike's volume off mute, and speaks the commentary.

Fiction or Nonfiction?

In deciding whether to tell your story as nonfiction or fiction, consider your answers to the four questions at the beginning of the chapter. They will direct your choices.

Reasons for Telling

Think first about your reason for wanting or needing to tell the story. What did you say in answer to question one at the beginning of the chapter? Your reasons for telling your story will guide your decision.

Workshop writer Marie felt driven to write about her year as an abused wife. She had intense, disturbing material, but she didn't know how to get at it. Examining the reasons she was compelled to write about it helped her know how to approach and shape her story.

"The year I was a victim haunts me," she said. "I've had counseling, but I don't feel healed. I think it'd be therapeutic to write about it."

Studies do show benefits to writing about painful experiences. Dr. James W. Pennebaker writes about the physical and psychological benefits of writing about traumatic events for just fifteen or twenty minutes a day for just a few days in a row. In an experiment at The University of Texas at Austin, one group of subjects wrote about traumas in their pasts and another group wrote about trivial events. Blood samples taken before the experiment and after four days of writing showed improved immune systems for those who'd written out their pain, a benefit that lasted a full six weeks. In a study at the State University of New York at Stony Brook, patients with asthma or arthritis wrote twenty minutes a day for three days; two-thirds wrote about the most stressful events in their lives and the other third wrote about their plans for the day. Four months later, 47.1 percent who wrote about the bad stuff had significantly improved physically, while only 24.3 percent of the daily planners improved. In fact, 21.6 percent suffered worsened conditions, while only 4.3 percent of those who'd written down their pain had gotten worse. So, patients, get out thy notebooks and heal thyselves.

Marie wanted to improve her psychological immune system. Writing nonfiction—the direct approach—seemed more likely to produce protective antibodies. Nevertheless, when she wrote about her husband's suspicions, paranoia, threats, and punching fists, she was frustrated with the resulting essay. It sounded defensive and whiny, and she didn't feel any better, either.

Why not? Writing as therapy limits a story's purpose and potential. Behind Marie's account of her year in marital hell ran a chant: *I was a victim, I was a victim, I was a victim.* Instead of feeling sympathy (much less empathy), readers found the writing self-pitying and angry. *Horrible him, poor me.*

"Marie," I said, faking my wise-teacher role, "let's extend the notion of writing as therapy. Instead of writing to get it out and get over it, try writing to understand it."

I quoted Maya Angelou: "If you are going to write autobiography, don't expect that it will clear anything up. It makes it more clear to you, but it doesn't alleviate anything. You simply know it better."

So instead of merely recounting the events and your feelings, I suggested, go deeper. Examine the dynamics, the underlying causes, all the complexities. This honesty will take great courage. I let Tobias Wolff help me out: " . . . a memoir is a tremendous instrument for understanding oneself and one's history, but you must be willing to acknowledge when your history wasn't what you wish it was."

Certainly Marie hadn't wished to be abused. She wasn't trying to write up her experience in perfumed rose-colored ink, but she was limiting her colors to black and white. She had a self-protective stake in keeping the roles simple: *you abuser, me victim.* That's what she wished her history to be.

"Marie," I said, "you don't have to write to say that domestic abuse is bad and wrong. You know that, your readers already know that. What you can do for yourself and for your readers is to go far and deep into the hidden labyrinth of the secret world of domestic abuse." Nonfiction allowed her to examine and discuss the complexities as fiction wouldn't, but first she had to give up writing for therapy and change her purpose. When she wrote to understand, she discovered, magically, the therapeutic side effects.

Initially, Marie had a second reason for wanting to write about abuse. "I want to help other women," she said. "I want to give them the courage to get out of abusive relationships." This purpose, however, was as limiting as the first. This time she was writing to cure others, but the goal was still therapy. Nonfiction was the way to go here as well, especially since she had information about legal resources and support services to pass on, but the writing tone was preachy. When Marie changed her purpose to understanding, she discovered another side effect: readers who were put off when she had an agenda were now inspired and moved.

Writers seeking to deal and heal ought to write instead for a higher (or deeper) purpose. And in most cases, nonfiction is more likely than fiction to lead them to understanding and its side effects.

In a personal essay called "Junkie Speak," Judy Plapinger wrote about the duality of her life "on heroin" and "after heroin." In alternating sections, she wrote scenes with people, details, and dialogue, and she wrote paragraphs that describe and comment. Here are a few sections:

> If I start in the middle, how will I ever begin? A good junkie doesn't clutter herself with questions like that. Beginnings are formed where the needle meets the vein. Endings are the dying of the bloodstream.

> Jeremy played to the crowd; I stood on the side of the riser. He leaned down and whispered to me, "Some things never change."

> "Yeah," I said. "Including us." But he was already back in front of the mike, and I was turning toward the bus station.

> Contradictions. Crosses and hexes and border towns. Melted by the heat, the hundreds of suns. Liquid residue cooked into indelible sunscreen lotion flows into my

bloodstream. Dire need for something to do, anything except what must be done. All I can anticipate is the discomfort and anxiousness of kicking, and the dullness and depression that follow. The drinking and the weight gain. The long, horrible, restless nights followed by the horrible, restless mornings which come too soon, when I'd give anything not to be awake, and when I'd give anything for a syringe filled with sleep and heroin. The rest of my life looks over my shoulder, tries to stay ahead of the sadness snapping at my ankles, laughing, sneering in the bleakness of my mind. I feel too unworthy of being well. How long can I be eye to eye with the abyss, and not blink, run like hell, take something?

On stage, Jeremy sang, "I don't have nobody to give my love to/And tonight you could peel me off these walls like wallpaper glue."

My language has changed. I remember again. This is not easy. I communicate too clearly and it scares people. So I stay inside and let the answering machine pick up my calls. RJ calls twice in two days. "Hey ho. Hi. This is me." His voice drawls a little Texas, a little methadone. "Just wanted to see how you're doing. Okay. Call me." Both messages use the same words spoken in the same intonation. The repetitiousness of junkie speak, so familiar it makes my head pound. I've tried to forget their phone number—I don't have it written down, but it doesn't matter because I remember everything now. No more blotted out spaces, chinks in chronology. Everything clicks like a clock face. Time drags down. Being clean isn't relevant. I'm still dirty. I wish I could let it go like a supernova—a brilliant explosion of ancient desperation.

The story's scenes, most of them longer than in this sample, might have been lifted from fiction. Plapinger might have chosen to write the whole story as fiction, letting the reader witness a stand-in character's life on heroin and after heroin. Instead, she rendered it as nonfiction and gained the chance to talk *about* the experiences, the sensations, and the feelings. In fiction, she'd have been limited, pretty much, to

showing the scenes and *suggesting* the feelings. In fiction she'd have mis-
led the reader into focusing on a plotline, into believing that the story
was about the various people who show up. In nonfiction, though, the
reader understands that the story isn't about Jeremy and the others, it
isn't about what happens, but it is about the condition of addiction and
its residue. In nonfiction Plapinger can ask questions ("How long can
I be eye to eye with the abyss, and not blink, run like hell, take something?"), she can make direct statements ("All I can anticipate is the
discomfort and anxiousness of kicking, and the dullness and depression that follow"), she can comment ("I communicate too clearly and it
scares people"), she can analyze ("Being clean isn't relevant"), and she
can let her own strong voice cry out ("Beginnings are formed where
the needle meets the vein. Endings are the dying of the bloodstream").
Nonfiction was a bold and wise choice.

Do you want to write so your stories—your life—can be handed down,
so they don't die without a trace, so your stories don't stay locked
within you? Again nonfiction is more likely than fiction to accomplish
that goal. A danger of writing for the grandchildren is the tendency to
sanitize the truth, and a danger of writing for posterity is to moralize
or sentimentalize. Here, too, you must go eyeball to eyeball with the
truth. Unblinking nonfiction can make you *heard*, solid in the world.
The story scrawls: *Kilroy was here*.

Some write to expose a wrong. The writer proclaims: I speak to you
from inside, I have lived this, and the world should know the truth.
Child abuse survivors, institutionalized patients, concentration camp
inmates—all those who have lived long enough to tell can give voice to
those who can't, can bear witness and testify to the truths from inside.
A danger is to write for self-justification, for revenge, or for blame.
A danger, again, is to rant, to write in stark black and white rather than
nuanced, complicated gray. But if they can expose the details in full,
careful honesty, whistle-blowers and survivors of horror should choose
nonfiction to proclaim their truths.

Some want to get a story out because they believe they have incredible
experiences. They want their true stories told, and as self-aggrandizing
nonfiction. At least twice a year I get a call or email from someone
with a fantastic story. She was trapped in a religious cult, he was set
up and framed by the DEA, she was abducted by aliens (no, really), he
was a roadie for a famous band, and she had an affair with a famous
author. They have great stories, but they're not writers and they need
help. I suggest classes where they can learn to write their stories. No,

what they want is for me to do it. They will give me the great gift of their material, I will spin it and weave it into a book, and when it hits the bestseller list, as it is certain to do, we'll split the profits 50-50. Of course, ghostwritten and as-told-to books sometimes do get published and do well in the marketplace, and not all of them sensationalize their stories. But every life owns a great story. "There are no dull lives," author Jay Parini pointed out, "only dull writers." The real story isn't merely the shocking events of a life: The real story is the unique voice of the storyteller coming to understanding and interpretation of the shocking events. Writing to exploit life experiences and to cash in on them practically guarantees a shallow, phony book.

Owning a great story (as any writer does) might lead some to write about it not to cash in but to take readers for the same ride. The story is an adventure, full of suspense. What will happen next? And then . . . ? Or another writer with Marie's material, for instance, might want to give readers the vicarious experience. Sadistic as that may sound, living the events with the narrator might lead to deeper emotional and psychological understanding of an abusive relationship than volumes of talk about it—for the writer as well as the reader. If your reasons for telling a story are to entertain or to rewrite events the way they *should* have happened, or to experience the events as a way to understand them, you should choose fiction. Giving your experience over to someone else, a character who may resemble you but isn't a clone, and unchaining scenes from facts free a story to discover its own truths.

My student Tyson Hudson wanted to write about social problems and family tensions on a Navajo reservation, but writing down his direct personal experience would be difficult. Examining joblessness and alcoholism in an essay might be safer, but it would keep them as abstract issues and would keep those caught up in the problems as mere case reports or statistics. So he wrote a short story showing a family in turmoil as seen through the eyes of the young son. The father, frustrated by being out of work and having to depend on his wife to make the money, feels guilty and angry. He's drinking (though he's going to AA meetings and trying not to). In addition, he carries bad Vietnam experiences with him even though he was a "hero." Finally, the little boy innocently allows his father to articulate this and to return home, literally but also figuratively. Here's the middle part of "The Silver Star":

> McGee woke late in the night. He heard his father and
> mother yelling. He turned on the night light next to his
> bed. He looked up from his bed and saw his Space Shuttle

Columbia poster shake. He put the pillow over his head, but he heard the angry voices still. He got up and went to his closet. He dug around in the dark until he found his black earmuffs. He put them on and walked into the living room. He saw his parents yelling at each other. He didn't understand what they were saying. They were arguing in Navajo, so he yelled, AHHHHH! Don't yell!

McGee sniffed and went back to bed. He pushed his earmuffs tight to his ears until he could hear only his breathing. Then he felt the walls shake. A moment later, the light turned on and his mother was at the door. She came up to him and he saw tears in her eyes. His mother leaned over and hugged him. I'm sorry, sha yhaz. You don't have to hear dat.

Later he heard a gun blast and dogs barking in the distance. McGee went out, fully dressed. He walked north, away from the floodlight until it was pitch black. He looked up and saw the stars. He pointed around with his right hand until he saw where his dad pointed out the Little Dipper. He followed one side of the constellation until he saw it. North Star, said McGee.

He walked in the dark for fifteen minutes. He looked around for skinwalkers and coyotes. He tripped over a sagebush and scraped his knee. As he got up, he saw a flash, and then heard a gun blast. He walked over to the flash and noise.

As he moved closer, the flash seemed to be coming from above. He walked quietly. When McGee got twenty yards away, he saw the flash was coming from a juniper tree. He walked slowly and carefully. He crouched behind sagebrush until he was five feet away. He looked up and heard someone loading bullets. McGee was cold and stiff. He looked around him and then he looked up and said, Dad! It's me!

He heard the juniper shuffle and then crack. He watched a branch and a tallboy of Bud fall to the ground and then his dad. His father said, Sonva bitch! Wha you doin' 'ere?

McGee walked backwards as his father got up. A flashlight turned on and it pointed at McGee.

Dad. I, uh, I was looking for you.

Come 'ere! his father demanded. He dropped his rifle and grabbed McGee by the arm and spanked him several times.

McGee started to cry and he sobbed, I'm sorry. I'm sorry. I was just—just looking, he sniffed. For you, Dad.

It's dangerous out 'ere, McGee. What if you got hurt? Or a bobcat eats you? Dammit, you should've stayed home with Mom.

You guys are always mad, McGee sobbed. You're always shooting your gun.

Ah shit. His father rubbed his face. Look. I'm just pissed off. His father kicked the empty tallboy. Well, pissed off an' . . . His father looked up at the night. I don't know, son. Things aren't good for now. Ever since the mines closed, it's hard. Your mom's been working two jobs and I got nothing. Just making jewelry and selling it for cheap. I—I don't know.

How come you're always shooting your gun? McGee sobbed.

His father was quiet for a minute and he said, I don't know. It makes me feel better. When I was away from your mom, I used—I used to go out all wasted an'—an' shoot my gun into the dark. Remember what I told you 'bout what's in the jungle?

McGee nodded.

He watched his dad staring at the rifle on the ground and then he looked up at the sky and said, Yeah. I don't know. At least it's better dan shooting someone or shooting yourself. McGee, I've seen some things that I hope you'll never see.

Dad? McGee asked.

Yeah?

I want to go home.

Yeah, okay.

Dad?

Yeah.

Are you okay?

McGee watched his dad look down at him. He messed up
his hair and said, Yeah, sure. Let's get outta 'ere.

Telling the story as fiction, through the eyes of a child, a naïve narrator who doesn't understand his parents' problems, allows the details
and dialogue of the scenes to reveal indirectly the dynamics of the family. The sparseness and apparent simplicity of the writing let the reader
walk in McGee's shoes, a quieter path to understanding than the noisy
highway of discussion, analysis, and commentary. Living the child's
story as fiction was risky but a right and moving choice.

So first and most important in deciding whether your story should
grow into fiction or nonfiction, consider your reasons for wanting to
write it. Your purpose will guide you.

Nothing But the Facts

A writer has an unwritten contract with the reader, and the document's clauses depend on the genre. Fiction's contract promises to let
the reader live the events of the story with a character. In the best one-
line definition I know, John D. MacDonald said fiction is "something
happening to somebody you have been led to care about." The reader
signs fiction's contract as co-creator.

Nonfiction's contract promises a different sort of intimacy between
writer and reader. The storyteller goes into the confessional to tell
secret truths, those truths that may be stranger than fiction, and the
reader listens and receives the confidences. The reader signs nonfiction's contract with a priest's expectation of the truth.

Do you know the facts of your story? Can you research them? Are
there ways to verify your memories? Memory is subjective, of course,
but if you can take an oath to factual accuracy and historical reality,
then nonfiction is safe in your hands and can proceed to interpret the
facts. Otherwise, allow memory and imagination to select and invent
the details and the people in the telling of the story.

Nancy E. Turner's first novel, *These Is My Words*, subtitled *The Diary of Sarah Agnes Prine, 1881–1901, Arizona Territories*, was inspired by an actual diary written by her great-great-uncle Henry Prine, brother-in-law of her great-grandmother. Turner did plenty of historical and family research, but it wasn't enough to reveal either the facts or the feelings of the real Sarah's life. When Turner switched to fiction, she wrote a story that rings as true as if it were not written but unearthed.

Related to the extent of the factual material is its sufficiency. "Fiction is condensed reality," author Alison Lurie wrote, "and that's why its flavor is more intense, like bouillon or frozen orange juice." If the reality is already rich enough in its own right, write the story as nonfiction. Otherwise, invent a shadow reality that is "realer" than the watery facts inspiring it.

The Voice of the Story

The most important element in the potency of a story is its voice. Whose voice relates the story? What is the sound of that voice: its rhythms, its accent, its expressions, its volume, its timbre, its variations on its theme?

Author Richard Bausch claims that every story depends "first and foremost on voice: whatever the argument may be, and no matter what else the work may be doing or trying to do, it must always rely on the sound of a voice—talking, breaking an implied silence or at least interrupting the random noise of our day." He's right. Thinking about whose voice should tell your story will guide your choice when you get to the fiction and nonfiction fork in the road.

If the voice that wants to speak the story is your own or one very much like what you hear in your head, what you use when you are alone, consider proceeding left into nonfiction. If the voice emanates from another throat, even if it sounds similar to one of your personal voices (who has only one voice, after all?), then take a right into fiction. If parts of the story want to be told by more than one speaker, turn right.

Writer Diane Doe began her novel with an authorial voice that knew a great deal more than did its main character. It wasn't a totally wimpy voice, but it explained too much. It got in the way of the story. Here's a part of the first incarnation:

> Streetlights spilled through the venetian blinds, flickering
> shadows across her bed. Her mother stood in the door-
> way, the hallway light behind her—hair spun up like a

honey-glazed donut, her eyes a piercing brown, her voice as always filled with an edge and particularly dangerous when it got syrupy. "Why aren't you sleeping?" she said.

Lila noticed her coat. The rhinestones twinkling on her ears. "I'm thinking."

"Expecting company?" Mika pointed to the chairs. Lila laughed nervously. She had placed three chairs at the foot of her bed in case any of the saints, Jesus, or Mary wanted to visit with her. The idea had come to her after waking from a bad dream and even though she hadn't formed an idea of what or who God was, she thought she'd better cover her bases just in case.

"You look pretty, Mom, what's up?"

Mika eyed her coolly. "That sounds like I don't always look pretty."

Lila felt as if she were being drawn into something she wouldn't get out of, like a bug stepping onto a spider's web.

What's wrong with this? Nothing, really. The writing is smooth, the scene is clear. Yet there's a distance here, caused by the writer's voice as intermediary. Doe gets in the way of the direct experience, explaining blatantly ("The idea had come to her after waking from a bad dream and even though she hadn't formed an idea of what or who God was, she thought she'd better cover her bases just in case") and subtly ("her voice as always filled with an edge and particularly dangerous when it got syrupy").

What would happen if Doe let the little girl Lila tell her story directly, in her own voice? Here's a sample:

My mom's brown eyes have fire in them or at least that's how it feels when she looks at me. Like a burn.

"What the hell are you doing, Lila?"

I pretend the mirror is ice and the heat of her words cools down and does not burn me.

"Never mind. Just get ready for bed." She presses her lips into a Kleenex and now her lips are on her face and the Kleenex. I think about how Veronica wiped the face of

Jesus while he was lugging that cross and how an imprint of his face stayed on the cloth. Kind of like the mirror but different.

"You look pretty, Mom."

"That sounds like I don't always look pretty."

I'm too far from the mirror to have her words cooled down so I walk to my bed. Maybe if my back is to her I'll be safe. The venetian blinds let light from the street move through the slats against my walls and ceiling. I look every night and sometimes see a guardian angel, but mostly blotches like the smeared ink tests they give you in the nut ward.

Mika is standing in the doorway of my room. I can see her from the corner of my eye. I grab my pajamas from under my pillow. Her hands are on her hips. Her mouth starts moving. "I'm going out, Lila, and I want you settled for the night." And I think maybe I'm some kind of stomachache that needs to be settled. I remember one of her boyfriends telling me about land mines. How you could just be walking along and step on one and be blown to pieces.

"Where are you going, Mom?"

"Why, are you my mother?"

"I don't know, Mom, am I?"

"Don't be smart, Lila."

"Are you going to see that doctor guy again? I like him the best."

"You're not dating him—so it doesn't much matter—does it? Now go to bed."

"What's his name? Tom?"

"Get ready for bed."

"I'm getting ready." I button my pajama top. "Is it a new guy?"

"Yes, he's new. For Christ's sakes."

"Can I meet him?"

"No, honey." She moves closer to me. This is when the lion grabs the zebra by the neck and snaps it broken just before he eats it. I saw it in a movie. A real movie. "He doesn't know I have a kid. You know." Her mouth is curved up and she is not yelling so I figure she's smiling.

I haven't brushed my teeth yet, but I plop into bed even though my pajama bottoms are still under my pillow. I figure we will stop talking if I'm in bed.

"Honey." She sits on the chair I have reserved for the Virgin Mary. "If Mommy's not home . . ." This is when I look around the room to see if maybe she's talking to someone else. She clears her throat. "You get yourself ready for school."

In this revision, Lila gets to speak for herself. This isn't a matter of first person (Lila as "I") versus third person (Lila as "she"). It has everything to do with the writer's hearing and writing down the voice that wants to tell the story.

Who should tell your story? You? Okay, let its voice be your own most lively and honest voice. Your stand-in? Okay, let its voice be bold and honest. A character's? Okay, let its voice be individual and quirky. A clear and vital voice leads to the truth of the story, whether it's nonfiction or fiction.

I'm Gonna Te-elll

Sometimes we want to tattle, but writing for revenge or to get someone else in trouble isn't exactly the most noble of motives and inhibits storytelling anyway.

More often, it's fear of hurting others that holds back our stories. Again and again I hear, "There's a certain story I want to write but can't until a certain person dies." When that certain someone finally shucks the mortal coil and frees the writer, it's too late. The compulsion has faded with time. Or, some discover, the compulsion unexpectedly evaporates when the tangled relationship underlying it disappears. Death has its own way of resolving some things. It's life that needs storytelling to find the truth.

Chapter two suggested strategies for getting around and getting over the fear of hurting others. Here I will not presume. This is your life. These are your loved ones, or the unloved ones you nevertheless must live among. Only you can decide how to walk your days before the shuffling off of your own coil.

However you write your true stories, as fiction or nonfiction, you will expose not only others but yourself. Only you can decide how transparent the words should be that clothe your stories.

But I will presume to remind us, you and me, that our pencil-wielding and keyboard-stroking days are finite. Let us find ways to tell our stories while we can.

Morphing Genres

The solution to the boredom of a fitness program featuring only one activity is cross-training, rotating several fitness activities. Cross-training benefits writers, too. Playing with different genres is great exercise to stretch writing skills and enliven your genre of choice. Author Mary Gordon said that fiction is "the love child of two deeply incompatible parents. It has journalism for a father, poetry for a mother." Whatever your particular love child is, experimenting with its parent genres will teach you techniques for raising a lively, intelligent kid.

The way to show yourself the different effects achieved with each genre is to morph a little story animal into three different creatures: nonfiction, poem, and fiction. Try this: Write a page about the weirdest job, paid or volunteer, you've ever had. Scuba diving in water traps for golf balls? Leading Mitch Miller sing-alongs in a state mental hospital? Driving girls who jump out of cakes to bachelor parties? Raising surgical maggots for "maggot therapy"? What's yours? Quickly fill a page with the details and incidents you remember. Don't worry about coherence or explanation.

1. Now shape the raw material into a page (at least) that might be part of your memoir. What led you to the job? What happened on the job? What exactly did you do? What was it like? How did you feel about it? How did it affect your life?

2. Next, working from both the initial shapeless page of free associations and the memoir page, extract details of the job or of an incident that happened on the job and drop them down on a page in something that looks like a poem. Think of your first two pages as a whole cooked fish. Lift out the fish's skeleton from the flesh. This skeleton is your poem. What details are lifted onto the page of the poem? Which parts remain, boneless, on the plate of prose? Keep rearranging the skeleton

until it leads you to a final line or pair of lines that say something surprising.

3. Return to the first raw page. Find mention of some specific incident that happened on the job. Write a scene showing what happened that particular time. Write it in first person, but immediately give the "I" a name (not your own). Give the other person or people in the scene new names, too. What are the characters doing? What do they say to each other? What unrelated thoughts come out of the blue into the narrator's head? Let go of what actually happened and let your narrator direct what appears on the page. The writer is conspicuously absent.

4. Follow up with written comments about how the experience of writing each piece differed. How was the process of writing the poem different from writing the page of memoir? How was your approach to writing the fictional scene different from writing the actual details and memories? From writing the poem? Reread all three pieces. Make some notes about how each one differs from the other two. What aspects of each one are especially effective? Which morphed creature has the most vitality? Why?

You can apply this exercise to the story you want to write, following the pattern: Freewrite, write the details of the facts as memoir, then lift out the skeleton into a poem, and finally try a fictional scene. The right genre choice will be revealed. Shazam!

Your own strengths as a writer can help make the decision about how to tell a story. Your reasons for wanting to tell the story will guide you, too. And the nature of the story itself has a say in the matter. Putting yourself on the witness stand and taking the oath to tell yourself the truth about these considerations will direct the story to the right form for telling the whole truth.

Listen to Me

Writing a blog can be another way of bending and blending genres. Blogs serve practical purposes such as marketing and audience-building, certainly, but most especially their popularity reminds me that writers simply want to be heard.

Australian writer Sherryl Clark is the author of dozens of books for children and teens—but her blog "Books and Writing" (sherrylclark.

blogspot.com) is her way of thinking out loud about reading and writing. "I like that no one can tell me what to write or how. I get very weary of the publishing world where everything is mostly out of my control."

For former newspaper editor and publisher Robert E. Cox, "Blogging allows me freedom to vent, or pass along an interesting or funny or sad factual story or an as-yet-undiscovered piece of my fiction without any restrictions, when the moment moves me. It's total independence—unlimited by space, growly (and too often clueless) editors, or timing, or whatever political correctitude is in vogue. It is a freedom to speak . . . And unlike the finality of newspapers, I can go back and change whatever I damn well choose to change" (www.oldgringosgazette.com).

Writer, editor, and university teacher Lee Skallerup Besette says that her blog "College Level Writing" (https://www.insidehighered.com/blogs/college-ready-writing/skills-inventory) changed her: "I am more engaged, more reflective, and perhaps, more militant, in my own small way. "

Warning 1: Maintaining a blog can be a distraction from other writing, a procrastination. Blogging can be time-consuming—and downright obsessive (respond to readers! check those stats!). So protect your other writing.

But the writing practice, the attentiveness to our lives, and the connections to readers can enhance our other stories.

Warning 2: Here you are your own editor. Though we write freely as we explore our stories, we revise, edit, and polish them before sending them out into the world for publication. This is my mini-rant about the sloppiness, in terms of spelling, grammar, and punctuation, of some blogs. Why would a writer take less care here? Advice: Read through a blog entry at least three times. Journalists are advised to wait fifteen minutes before posting. The rest of us can afford to wait a little longer.

What makes a good blog? Sherryl Clark likes blogs that are "thoughtful and interesting and present ideas and information." She adds: "I don't read blogs that get too self-indulgent (navel gazing)."

What makes a good blog? "Strong opinion, clearly stated, based on fact, or logic, or reasonable presumption," Robert E. Cox notes. "Good blogs, as any literature, are written by people who don't care what others think, who are not afraid to express their opinions, and who never lose a second of sleep worrying about the fallout."

What makes a good blog? The same qualities that hold for all our stories: courage, bold writing, strong voices. Listen to me.

7

SPLASHING IN THE ABYSS:
APPLYING SPECIAL TECHNICAL TIPS

I learned how to scuba dive in a swimming pool. My open-water dive for certification was in a rock quarry in Illinois in March. Thirty feet down in the water, shivering in a thick, ill-fitting wetsuit, I could not see my hand three inches in front of my mask. All of my lessons from the clear pool vanished. The quarry water was so dense, it became another element—or it became all of the elements, fire and wind and earth mixed into the black water. Submerged in the tumult, I could not tell up from down. Where was the surface? Where was the shore? Which way was the bottom? Where was the divemaster? I was alone and blind, biting into a rubber mouthpiece straining to deliver fake oxygen. This was the full panic of the grave, turning within the heavy vacuum.

Since then, I have gone diving in water so clear the manta rays and I flew through it. I have knelt on white sand with my hands out and dolphins have swooped down to rub against my palms. I have played with sea lion pups in a silt-shimmering cave. Somehow, buried alive in the quarry, I knew it would be worth it, and I willed myself into stillness and let the elements turn around me. I pretended I could breathe. At last, someone put a rope in my hand and towed me to the surface. I burst through into the late winter Midwestern air. "Wow, oh wow! Wasn't that great?" the divemaster whooped. "Yes," I said around the mouthpiece. And it was, not only because I had faked it long enough to gain entry into the blue glory to come, but because now I was intimate with the abyss.

Swimming Pool Lessons

When I was young, the other kids claimed the quarry was bottomless, a belief backed up by our parents' warnings not to play there. So, of course, we had to sneak out and climb down the hill to the rocky shore. It was equal parts tantalizing and terrifying. We went in wearing our Keds and none of us waded in beyond our knees, for who knew what had been spawned in the depths.

Once you've taken the plunge and lived to ascend, the abyss isn't so terrifying. You can pretend to know what you're doing down there. Breathe, you tell yourself, just breathe. You can remember that you were as intrigued by what you might find as you were scared.

On that first vertiginous dive, I hadn't really forgotten the swimming pool lessons. I knew little tricks—the best thing to prevent your mask from fogging is spit—and I knew bigger tricks—how to equalize ear pressure, how to clear a flooded mask, how to buddy breathe.

Splashing in the shallows helps you practice your technique. Here we'll look at technical tips that will help you write your stories and will lend them professional polish. These pool lessons will be available once you're down deep, whether you're consciously recalling them or not. Lessons of craft can be tested and refined only in the depths, and you will find the abyss isn't really bottomless.

Voice

I've said it before and I'll say it again: The single most important element in storytelling is voice. A clear and vital voice is what leads to the truth of the story and gives the writing authority.

I can tell you that a strong voice depends on specific details, on the narrator's particular choice of details, on such close proximity between writer and narrator that they are virtually one, on exaggeration, and on honesty. But "strong voice" is tricky to define and has as many manifestations as people have fingerprints.

Yet we know it when we hear it.

Here is the opening to a timid story (set pre-mobile phone):

> Because I can't seem to say no, I'm one of those people who are always helping others. At the apartment complex I manage north of Phoenix, we would not normally extend phone privileges to the public. Yet I cannot find a way to refuse the man in business clothes who knocks on the door and says that his car has broken down in the desert. Though I allow him to use the telephone, I try to keep my eye on him.

> My neighbor Mrs. Sanchez and her daughter Sonia are
> outside. If anything happened, they would hear through
> the window that I keep open a little bit for the air.
>
> It is not right to listen in on a conversation; nevertheless,
> the man is speaking loudly and I cannot help hearing.

The setup is interesting: Something is going to happen, for sure, and the man is going to be trouble. Beyond that curiosity, there's little to interest a reader. The bland, explanatory, sometimes formal language suggests little about the narrator. Compare my lame rewrite with the real opening to Katherine Salas's "Sugar":

> I'm always doing for people on account of I can't say no.
> Normally we do not extend phone privileges to the pub-
> lic but how can you turn away a man in business slacks
> whose car has just broken down in the desert sun some
> miles north of the city of Phoenix? While he's making
> the call I keep a close watch near the front door. Out the
> kitchen window I see Mrs. Sanchez and Sonia in the play-
> ground. I figure if he starts any funny business they'll hear
> me call out. I always keep the kitchen window cracked for
> the draw anyways.
>
> I don't mean to listen in on the conversation but how can
> you stop yourself from understanding plain English?

The information and the setup, with its built-in uh-oh factor, haven't changed. But the voice shifts the curiosity from the outsider to the speaker, Sugar, someone we're already getting to know, for a much more compelling opening.

Writer Frances P. Harris began her story "The Neighborhood" with a workshop prompt. She had a main character, Sylvia, who fit with the assignment, but pretty soon one of the observers of the main character took over. Harris described the process: "I saw YaYa as brown-skinned and around seventeen years old, but her other physical and mental attributes emerged as other characters interacted with her. My career as a Speech-Language Pathologist working with people with a variety of limitations and restrictions likely informed the shape of YaYa, but this was not intentional. YaYa's complexity is a good example of why one should not judge another based on a single attribute, and I wanted that to become clear through the scenes in the story." (And, I add, why writers must allow the people in their stories to be more than case studies or single-trait types, for better or worse.) That complexity is revealed through YaYa's voice:

> The last house on the block takes the whole corner and it is red brick with white columns and white shutters and two chimneys. It has azalea bushes and camellia bushes and gardenias that smell in the spring, and hydrangea that make different colors and five oak trees and on the back, the piney woods start and in the piney woods are blackberry bushes. In this house, I work. In this house, I came as a baby with Mama. In this house, I listen, and in this house the time moves so slowly when I am inside and I can hear the big clock ticking, then I go outside and the time moves fast then the day is over, and I walk down the street past all the houses so I can catch the bus on time and go back to shanty town and eat potatoes with green beans all smashed so's I can get it in my mouth and swallow okay and paw won't look at me — says I look like a bird needs worms, then I go out on the porch and smoke a pipe and it fits just right into my small mouth and I think about the sun going down and the cicadas buzz, buzz, buzz, and children run around chasing each other and I feel the pipe on the inside of my mouth with my tongue. And the night will come before I want it and then the morning and I will drink some milk from a straw. Mama says I will die soon. She must have said it for the last seventeen years and then she says I'm a miracle child and that's what the preacher says, that God saved me from dying as a baby for a reason. Said the good Lord made my head like a little bird, and my body like a little bird to remind us about the good life and the good Word and sometimes he points to me in church and says, Hallelujah, praise the Lord, praise Jesus for His pure love. Only I wonder about the Good Lord when I choke and choke but my pipe, it smells so sweet in the air. And in the morning, it will be another day on the calendar and I will eat a peach after I peel it and cut it up and smush it. I will eat a peach with my fingers or the baby spoon that Miss Sylvia gave

> me. Miss Sylvia, she says that she will go home soon,
> but she has been saying that for as along as I remember
> and the twins, they will grow up and stop thinking about
> me, and maybe the houses will change color, maybe the
> bushes will die and new ones will be planted and maybe
> Mrs. Forsythe will marry Mr. Chandler and they will live in
> her house because it has more rooms and maybe Daddy
> can work in the gas station and maybe Mama and Daddy
> will have a new baby, one that can eat right and run and
> play and do a day's work for a day's wages. And I rock in
> the rocking chair, and I go forward, then backward, then
> forward, then backward.

YaYa's voice comes through in the details she notes, her descriptions, and certainly the repetitions and the run-on rhythms of her sentences.

National Book Award–winning poet Ai was a master of voices. Her poems give voice to "characters" ranging from J. Edgar Hoover to Jimmy Hoffa to Elvis Presley. Listen to these voices kicking off poems in *Greed*: "A man needs ammunition." "Leave your porkpie hat on, lover." "I wasn't wearing anything but my underwear." "The smell of formaldehyde fills the car." "My wife deserved to be shot." These bold voices are persuasive and irresistible.

We hear a voice through its expressions, its rhythms, its sometimes ungrammatical or overly casual sentences. The boldness of a voice depends on exaggeration. Every voice should say, as does the speaker in Ai's poem "Self Defense": "Y'all listen to me."

Speaking in Tongues

A story is as much about its speaker as it is about its events, whether it means to be or not. There's no hiding. Even a weak voice that tries to mask its nature reveals the truth, unmasking the speaker as timid or self-serving or duplicitous.

Talking about voice is a roundabout way of talking about point of view. Fiction writers ponder point of view more than poets or nonfiction writers, getting tangled in first-, second-, or third-person voices; in omniscient, or limited, or fly-on-the-wall possibilities. But point of view isn't a matter of pronouns. It has everything to do with who is speaking. Whether it's the writer's voice or a character's voice (in poetry, the voice is often a special version of the writer's, but sometimes it's the voice of a person other than the writer), what the reader sees and hears and guesses depends on the voice relating the story.

To prove it to yourself, try this quick exercise:

1. Picture your bedroom. Jot down details of what you see in your mind's eye.

2. Your mother or father has just stepped into your bedroom. What does she or he notice? What does he or she say?

3. A two-year-old wanders into your bedroom. A lot lower to the floor than the rest of us and with different interests, the child pays attention to . . . what?

4. A puppy finds its way to your bedroom. Generally, I'd be wary of writing from an animal's point of view, but to make the point here, write down what the cute little guy sees and does.

5. An extraterrestrial's very first trip to Earth features a visit to your bedroom. How does it see things?

It's the same room, but its reality shifts according to who's doing the seeing. The details are the same, but certain objects stand out while others are practically invisible. How the room is described (messy? wonderfully quirky? smelly? soft? forbidding?) depends on the attitude of the beholder.

Whose voice should tell your story? The angle of vision, the mind-set, and the personality of your narrator (even if the speaker is you) will determine the selection of details, the way they're described, and the spin given to scenes. The particular voice telling your story is key to revealing its truths.

Back when she was my student, writer Shannon Cain began "The Village Ladies" this way:

> For more than seventeen years, Mamma Louisa had not set foot inside Francesca's home. Each woman in Villafelice di Fitalia had her own pitiful misfortune, each story a public one—how could it not be public in a place like this? But the disaster that kept Louisa away from her daughter-in-law had the irresistible element of scandal, not like the ordinary tragedies like a wife dead in childbirth or legs broken by hay wagons that tipped over on the steep hillsides where the crops grew.

"Mamma Louisa is our problem, not theirs," Immanuella was saying to Francesca as she eased the pasta into the boiling water. "Their tongue wagging is of no concern to us." It was an ancient Sicilian protection mechanism, born of centuries as a defeated, conquered people. First the Greeks invaded the island, then the Romans, then the Turks followed by just about every other civilization from northern Africa. All we can do, goes the theory, is mind our own business, shrug our shoulders and ignore the outsiders trying to kill us with their swords and demoralize us with their lies.

Imma was repeating an old speech, and Francesca knew she would not expect a reply.

This opening promises a good tale in an exotic setting. But there is something about the storytelling voice—almost a voice-over—that keeps the story in the past and in a distant place. Look what happens when Francesca herself speaks, in the opening of "Amore Saffico":

You know there is a secret about me, don't you. I can see it in your eyes. They surely haven't told you what it is. You must have learned bits and pieces, as children do, pretending to play with their dolls but paying close attention when the adults' conversation sounds interesting.

Dear girl, dear grandchild, I thought I would never meet you. Your mother, my ungrateful Filomena, she left so angrily when she was almost as young as you are now, and she never looked behind her. Never brought her children back to see their grandmother. I think she married your father simply because he promised to take her away from this place. She must be itching with curiosity about what has become of me. You can tell her I am just fine, thank you very much. Not dead yet. She should be more patient.

Well, then. Do you see the church, there? It is the church of my childhood. The church where I was baptized, had my first communion, confessed my transgressions, and got married. The church where my funeral will be held. This was the church I ran away from, on that day— *Madonna!*—more than fifty years ago.

This time we hear the story from the inside, and its material is transformed from scandalous gossip into passionate confession.

If the speaker of your story-in-progress is unidentified, more a voice-over than an integral part of the action, then put those pages aside. Just as an experiment, don't look at them and write the same scene again, this time in the private voice of the major participant (who may be you). Let this bold voice sing out. I can almost guarantee that the story, even if it happened fifty years ago, will have the engaging immediacy that makes people and events matter to readers.

It's All About You

Memoirs and personal essays are typically written in first person, the "I" of the author's angle of vision. Occasionally, I've seen passages shift to second person, the "you" who becomes the disassociated "I," perhaps as the author simultaneously looks at and looks away from an intense experience. Short stories and novels are typically written in first person or in third person singular—the angle of vision of the "he" or "she" narrating the story. (Every now and then, a fiction writer pulls off the experiment of first-person plural narration, such as Joshua Ferris in *And Then We Came to the End* or Andrea Barrett in *The Air We Breathe.* In these books, it was absolutely essential that "we" tell the story.) Fiction writers also have the choice of second person, angles of vision that are both a stand-in for "I" and an invitation—no, a command— for the reader to participate. See stories in Junot Diaz's *This Is How You Lose Her* for fearless examples.

Second person insists on exaggeration, on specific detail, and on a bold voice.

When writer Estella Gonzalez needed a way to explore strong material, she turned to second person:

How to Talk to Your Mother

Wear your breast plate.

The heart is the first thing

she'll go for, then your eyes

so keep your visor down.

Make sure you wear thick

gloves and carry a whip. She'll

come at you with claws drawn,

ready to slash your mouth.

Bury your words in a ball of cheese

like that pill you feed your cat.

She'll chew on your story

before she chokes and spits.

Before you know it, blood will splatter

on the apple blossom wallpaper.

Her tongue, torn at the base

will wag, wiggle,

lick your lips.

Put her tongue in a jar,

just to be safe,

just until you're ready

to make a break for your car,

to lock the doors,

to secure the safety belt.

Run right over her raggedy

dog, the one with the sad eyes

who bit your boob

when you turned 15.

Thanksgiving, Christmas,

and don't forget Mother's Day,

repeat as necessary.

Gonzalez said, "The idea of an instruction manual for daughters in conflicted relationships with mothers struck me as helpful and funny."

Voice Lessons

Try your own instruction manual. Fill in the blank with someone you have conflicted feelings about: "How to Talk to Your _____." Boss, sister, ex, son, teacher . . . Be bold. Exaggerate. Be downright outrageous.

Writing as "you" will be liberating. Playing with second person instills lessons that will carry right over as you create strong first- and third-person voices.

Other Voices

One of the pleasures of reading is the chance to eavesdrop on conversations and arguments: what the pair behind you on the airplane say, the secret a woman in a public bathroom tells her friend (not knowing you're in a stall), what you hear when you listen through the glass held up against the motel room wall (oh, sorry, I know you've never done that).

Whether the writer is re-creating remembered conversations or putting words into characters' mouths, dialogue brings scenes to life. Though I often hear writers complain that they struggle to write good dialogue, it's as much fun for the writer as it is for the reader. Try the following exercises, and you'll see what I mean.

He Said, She Said (Take 1)

Two people are at a mall together. They may be a couple, friends, or parent and child. They may be the same or different gender—whatever, that's up to you. One person notices that the other one keeps scoping people out. As they wander into stores and around the food court, what do they say? Set the scene in motion and see what they say to each other.

Writing the mall scene will show you these techniques for writing dialogue:

- Effective dialogue isn't real. If you transcribed an actual conversation, you'd find it full of fillers and inconsequentials. Instead, you want the illusion of real talk. The best way to know whether what's on the page sounds real is to read it aloud. Try your argument (and I'll bet it did turn into an argument, no matter how mildly it began) out loud. What mere space-filler comments can be cut? How can lines that don't quite sound real be rephrased?

- To create the illusion of real talk, mimic the ways people talk: short sentences, usually, or incomplete sentences; interruptions (impolite, maybe, but real); contractions (not "I do not think she is so hot" but "I don't think she's so hot"); and individual verbal tics, accents, and expressions. Remember, it's the illusion we're after, so keep a light touch on dialect. Read back through your mall dialogue. Is it too tidy? Have you allowed your people to interrupt each other and to be mean?

- Every piece of dialogue needs a reason to exist. Every line should add to the reader's knowledge of the situation, the people, the events, the relationships, or the feelings. Dialogue that merely gives information or description is better turned into direct narration—not "Look over there at that window display featuring mannequins in fluffy pink lingerie," but "'Honey, don't look.' She pointed at the store window mannequins in fluffy pink lingerie." What lines in your mall dialogue are static and could be cut? Does each remaining line somehow push the scene forward?

- Real talk is messy, as should be the illusion of real talk on the page. People don't always answer each other's questions directly. He: "Do you want a Coke with your pizza?" She: "I saw the way you were looking at her." People don't reply with the expected response. She: "You want diet or regular?" He: "Why would you ask *that*?" Do the pair in the mall dialogue answer each other with non-sequiturs sometimes? That's good.

- Real talk isn't coherent, so the illusion shouldn't be too neat, either. People talk about more than one thing at a time. They move on to a new topic and loop back. Conversation is like counterpoint. He: "Let's go check out the games." She: "My mother doesn't like you, you know." In your mall dialogue, is each party singing a separate melody with occasional convergences? Good.

- Real talk doesn't happen in a vacuum, and the illusion on the page, as well as the pacing, will be enhanced when scenes happen somewhere, when the speakers are engaged in some stage business. Is your dialogue balanced with mall details and your pair's actions?

- In real life, people don't always say what they mean. Instead, they say the opposite, or they avoid the subject, or they dance around it. In story writing, this indirection reveals feelings, needs, and attitudes far better than blunt directness. In the mall scene, what do the pair say that they don't really mean? What do they leave unsaid? What subtext runs beneath the words they speak?

- Effective dialogue doesn't need the help of "said" substitutes or adverbs stating how the lines are delivered. *"Look at the woman on those jugs,"* he quipped, *pointing at the pottery in the antique store window. "Get the hell away from me," she growled angrily.* Writing appears more professional when people simply say their lines, rather than breathe, croak, snarl, hiss, wheeze, chortle, spit, gasp, sigh, muse, or expostulate them. (In the olden days, people were allowed to ejaculate their lines. Readers now have gotten prudish about such excess.) Adverbs attached to dialogue often lend the accidentally humorous effect of Tom Swifties—"I had a hot dog for lunch," said Tom frankly—even if they aren't puns. The trick is to get the line of dialogue right so that it can stand alone, with nothing but a virtually invisible "said."

- Often the speaker attribution can be omitted altogether: *"I don't believe it."* He pointed at the waiter in the rooster hat. *"That's my grandfather."* Sometimes inserting the speaker attribution in the middle of dialogue can neatly suggest a pause: *"I can't believe it,"* he said, *"but that guy in the rooster hat is my grandfather."*

He Said, She Said (Take 2)

Here's an exercise in dialogue, pacing, and subtext that you can do alone or with other writers:

1. On separate scraps on paper, name three activities that one or two people could perform, such as gutting a fish, changing the

oil, bathing a cat, shooting hoops, or diapering a baby. Drop the papers into a bag.

2. On separate scraps of paper, name three arguments a pair of people might have: a father and son arguing about curfew, partners arguing about bills, two sisters arguing about putting their mother in a nursing home, a teacher and student arguing about a grade. Drop the papers into a second bag.

3. Shake up the bags. Each writer takes one scrap of paper from each bag. The mission, no matter how impossible it seems, is to write a scene in which the pair from bag two have their argument while performing the action from bag one. Take no more than twenty minutes.

4. Read the scenes aloud. What makes them so effective (and I guarantee they will be)? How did opposing the argument's topic to the activity enhance pacing? Increase tension? Allow dialogue to suggest the pairs' real feelings (despite what they actually said)? What surprises showed up? Sometimes the most bizarre combinations lead to the best scenes.

Beginnings

A story on the page is like a house where a party is going on. The reader enters the story by opening the front door (no knocking necessary). The party is already in progress. Nobody introduces the new guest. The partiers are too far gone already. There's a drunk in the kitchen, an argument in the living room, a pair kissing in a bedroom. The reader begins by stepping into the middle of the story, at a critical point perhaps, just before the neighbors' complaints bring the police pounding on the door.

As we begin writing a story, we don't know what all is going to happen or who is going to show up, so we get started however we can. We spend three pages making canapés and cleaning the house. And that's okay. Later, though, we delete those pages and find the true beginning.

Here are some opening lines from my students' fiction and nonfiction that simply open the door on their stories:

Ray disliked Susan more than any human being alive, yet her naked body was thrusting against him at that very moment. —"The Lawn Mower," Ron Ries

A rhinoceros lumbered onto the road, and I had to swerve out of the way to avoid hitting the damn thing. —"Beasts," Matt Dinniman

I'm wearing my sister today. —"I'm Wearing My Sister," Joy Valerius

I think the thing I hate most about the frat boys is the way they smell. —"Circle K," Rachael Cupp

"I thought every woman wanted a baby," says Steve. —"Shayna," Jennifer Fernelius

Me and my friend, Sonny Ray, was walking down the embankment, beside the eastbound lane of I-10, looking for good stuff, when I saw this dead guy sitting under a mesquite tree. —"A Brave and Wondrous Thing," J.R. Dailey

My mother used to call the sleep of adolescent girls a state of bliss. —"Junkie Speak," Judy Plapinger

I stole the money from the cash box to buy sour-balls and a magazine that I thought would make me more intellectual. —"Leaving My Mother," Jennifer Colville

That bastard, it's almost time for him to come again, to slobber over me like a dog. —"Dancing Woman," Janet Smith

How could you not read on? These lines simply open their stories' doors. They don't announce themselves, they don't offer introductory paragraphs, they don't start three years (or even three minutes) earlier. They simply open the door. The scene is already in progress.

In addition, they offer bold voices and a sense of intrigue. In each one, you know something is going to happen. And it's probably not going to be good, either.

Middles

Something's already happening when we open the door to the story, and after that things really go bad. Whether this is a story of fistfights and crashing lamps in the living room or of quiet confession in the back bedroom among the piled-up coats, each scene serves to advance the story somehow. Sometimes it seems actions and talk are present only to get from one scene to the next: Instead of going forward, they just lie there flat, taking up space. The solution is to remove them but leave the space, to skip a line and cut to the next scene.

Sometimes the story goes forward by going backward. The flashback is a scene (not a quick memory or summary of a past event), complete with details, actions, dialogue, and thoughts. Like any other scene, it should reveal something new. A warning: If a flashback takes over a story, it almost certainly *is* the story and deserves to be accorded its full space and direct forward motion. Another warning: If flashbacks take up half the space, consider placing them at the story's beginning, in chronological rather than backward order.

Getting in and out of flashbacks can be dicey, leading to bad lines such as these:

The pounding of the construction worker outside the classroom reminded me of the pounding headache I'd had that summer when my favorite dog died.

I was startled back into the present when my mother thumped my head with her beer stein.

Simple cues can help: *When I was five* or *Now* . . . Otherwise, trust the power of white space and just make the jumps through time.

Back at the party, all hell's broken loose. A face has been slapped, awful words that can never be taken back have been uttered, a secret has been revealed. Push the scenes forward to the terrible or wonderful moment of truth, after which there's no going back.

Endings

At the end of the story, the reader simply exits by the back door. The party's not over, but the host is not-so-subtly carrying glasses to the kitchen. One of the kissers is crying, the drunk's passed out in the bathtub, the arguers are silently loading the dishwasher. Things have happened, and nothing is quite the same.

It's hard to know, sometimes, how to end a story. So we throw in a big surprise or clever twist, leaving the reader feeling manipulated or cheated, as if the invitation was to a New Year's Eve party that changes into a birthday party for poodles. Here are a couple that my students wrote as jokes:

"And as I looked around my new world, I understood that my life would never be the same, inside this sock drawer."

"And as I fell from the bridge to my death, my final thought was, I forgot to turn off the stove."

Desperate to end a story, writers might decide just to kill the character, a temptation that should nearly always be resisted. Or we keep going with a summarizing paragraph explaining the lessons learned, or with an epilogue showing where the players are five years later. That's okay, but when we finally run down, we can go back and locate the true ending—when it's time to walk out and close (or click or slam) the door behind us.

In my colleague Cynthia Arem's "The Cul-de-Sac Gang," a woman sneaks out at night to spray paint graffiti on her neighbors' houses. She isn't sure which of her nasty neighbors or their tormenting children has painted her front door with white curlicues while she was out, so she means to get even with all of them. The next day, rumors and accusations fly. The neighbors' secrets come out and the narrator learns something about herself as well. Here's the ending Arem wrote first:

> "Aunt Mary, I never sprayed that red paint. Someone else did, you gotta believe me, it wasn't me," Juli said. "Please don't send me home, please."
>
> "You're going," Mary said.
>
> "It's all your fault. If you didn't hate your neighbors so much this wouldn't have happened," Juli screamed.
>
> I backed toward the front door. As I opened it, I heard Mary crying. "I'm sorry, Phyllis, I'm real sorry," she said.
>
> Ruth Jackson was true to her word. She wouldn't let her son play with Michael Hamilton again. But she went a step farther. Within six months she divorced Mr. Tyrant and got some good counseling for herself and John. Michael Hamilton stopped lashing out at my son, Tommy, and even tried to protect him at the playground at school. Mr. and Mrs. Righteous eventually moved out of the neighborhood. As for me, I decided a bit of mischief can really have its benefits.

The final paragraph here went beyond the story's true ending to wrap things up too neatly, counseling included. And it wasn't true to the story, with its smug, platitudinous last sentence. Here's how the PEN prize–winning version of the story ended, following Juli's accusation:

> I backed toward the door. As I opened it, I heard Mary crying. "I'm sorry, Phyllis, I'm real sorry," she said.
>
> From Mary's porch I could see the curlicue lines on all three houses. I sort of liked them. We were all marked, as if we were part of the same gang.

The quieter ending shows that Phyllis has changed from her judgmental self into someone who sees the common humanity in the neighborhood. Your story, whatever its genre, may also want to shut its exit door quietly but firmly with a suggestive statement, like Arem's. Readers will get the message, though you haven't explained it.

Sometimes, though, what might look like tacked-on explanation is actually the story's fulfillment. The narrator's new understanding needs the words. In my student Sarah Flaten's story "About My Mother," a woman returns home to meet her mother's newest husband. In the course of the visit, old bad times are revisited, and both mother and daughter tell some secrets. Here's the final paragraph:

> I sat back at the table with a fresh cup of coffee. I had never known those things about my mother. And from the look in her eyes, I don't believe she had ever said any of it out loud. I felt a bit light. I knew I was no longer a child unknown by her mother. Not that she knew me now. That was just no longer who I was. And my mother had taken some shape in my mind. I could see a bit of her for the first time. She was just another person, and a girl, unknown by her mother. She was a woman who had been searching for a long time, but couldn't seem to find love. And a mother who didn't know her own child, and a woman who only half knew herself. But who had managed, somehow, to give me maybe just a little more than she got. And I think that maybe, maybe that's okay.

Here the narrator is given the space to contemplate her experience. Your short story, or especially your essay or memoir, can effectively conclude with a discussion of your new understanding, what connections you've made, or a meditation on the meaning of the experience.

Structure

One of the most frequent concerns I hear from beginning and struggling writers is that they can't figure out how to structure stories. All of their examination of published writing and reading of advice books haven't answered the big question of how to put together or shape the story they want to write. They believe they must know how to do it and what it will be before they can even begin to write the story.

I've put off talking directly about structure until now because you should (mostly) put off thinking about structure until after you've written a draft or two. Stories need structure, of course. Usually it's impossible to plan in advance. Your story line won't be plotted out before the journey: The map is made as you go.

In the writing, remember that the story is just one scene after another. It's almost that simple. It's like a play: Write scene one, drop the curtain, here's scene two in another time or place, drop the curtain, time for scene three, and soon you have a story (or, not quite as soon, a book).

Afterward look to see if each scene accomplishes its two main needs: Does it have tension? Does it somehow push the story forward? Try graphing the scenes. Your graph might follow the famous Gustav Freytag's triangle or pyramid: a conflict that quickly escalates in rising action, culminating in a climactic moment, followed by a short wrap-up. Poor Gustav, stuck in the nineteenth century and famous for his pyramid. Still, he was onto something. I once heard a feminist literary theorist complain that this design was too masculine for the likes of the twenty-first century: all projectile and explosion. She proposed alternate designs such as the way some of Alice Munro's masterful stories weave two strands together. Still, there is a helix rising, and the entwined strands both heighten in tension until something happens, something changes.

Your story will have an arc: first a hint of something wrong or about to go wrong, then tension escalates and things go wrong, things get even worse until something happens, some awful or great moment after which nothing will be the same, and then you can wrap it up. That's overly simplistic and there are many variations, but the theme is tension, increased tension, and release. I like to think this is a feminine as well as a masculine design: It's a human design.

Especially if you're approaching a larger project than a short story, a poem, or an essay, it helps to have some temporary structure on which to hang your scenes. It might be a clothesline on which you pin those scenes in chronological order (plus there are those handy spaces between clothespins).

Any artificial design, in the beginning, will help you write the book. Should you tell the story in chronological order? If there's no reason not to, then yes. There may well be reasons to design it otherwise. You might begin at the climactic moment and then backtrack to its lead-up. What's important—what happened or why it happened? Of course readers want to know both, but the design of the book might be directed by the answer.

My novel *Meridian 144* was a real mess of backward memories and forward story line until I imposed a plan: Chapter one would be the first day on the island after the nuclear holocaust and also the character Kitty's childhood, told in flashback; chapter two would be the second day of survival on the island and flashbacks to Kitty's adolescence;

chapter three . . . well, you get the idea. In the final chapter, the imme-diate story and the past story merge. Though the book got chopped up into shorter chapters and my scheme probably isn't apparent to readers, making this pattern helped me control my oceanful of material.

It doesn't matter if the final version adheres to the preliminary plan. Anything that will get the story out and onto the page is useful. You'll rearrange and reshape in the next draft anyway, thinking of scenes that increase tension and advance the story. Again, if there's no reason not to, just set it down in chronological order: This happened first, then this, and, oh boy, then this, and wait'll you hear this. . . .

Writing scenes in chronological order can benefit a book, even if you intend to move them around later. Writing the childhood scenes, for instance, first affords the deep advantages of helping you know what formed your character, what must be come to terms with, how the kid connects to the adult. Writing the early scenes in chronological order has the second advantage of granting them immediacy. Later you can move those scenes to their right places.

Of Refraction and Diffusion: Poetry Lessons

In poetry's special medium, vision changes the way it does underwa-ter. The diver wears a mask to provide an air space between eyes and water, allowing sight. The air space makes objects appear to be a third larger and distances a quarter closer than the actual object. The shape of a poem, so different from prose, is a sort of air space, so that light rays are bent as they pass from the dense material into refracted mean-ing. In poetry, objects and distances are bigger and closer than reality.

Underwater, visibility depends on the turbidity of the water, the choppiness of the surface, the stratification of the water into layers, the silt and plankton suspended in the water. The poem also depends on such conditions: the denseness, the roughness of the material, its layers of clarity, the residue that deflects and distorts the material, and how much truth is reflected and never directly enters the poem.

Even in clear water, 75 percent of light rays are diffused in the first couple dozen feet down. As the poet goes deeper into the material, which scattered and mingled details survive? Sunlight is a composite of all colors, but water filters the colors. Reds are absorbed first, then oranges, then yellows, then only greens and blues, until finally there's only black. Below a hundred feet, nearly all color except blue may be scrubbed. How can the poem use this absorption of irrelevant details to get to the true-blue truth that remains?

Most of this chapter, though it talks about prose, applies nearly as much to poetry. Here are some of poetry's special approaches that prose writers can borrow. I'm not playing genre favorites, but perhaps poetry can reveal our stories and their profound meanings in ways that dense prose can't always. And paying attention to these poetry lessons will help prose writers think about their stories, too, especially in terms of language, sound, voice, and structure. How much should be stated outright? How much should be suggested? How can imagery reveal what is too complex for mere words? How can your story speak the unspeakable? Poetry's lessons can lead you to answers, no matter what your genre of choice.

Image = Truth

The poet is deeper underwater than the prose writer. The poet is most concerned with the distorted or distilled image. The prose writer tells the story in scenes; the poet tells the story in images. I wonder if haiku, the epitome of show-don't-tell, can be seen as the ultimate lesson. The poet presents a no-comment picture to express and evoke emotion. The poet is the photographer: not always directly in the picture, but the one who took the shot, chose it, and maybe Photoshopped it. Present and (un)accounted for.

The eighteenth-century haiku master Buson was also a famous painter, so it's not surprising that his poems rendered vivid pictures of the world around him. This word picture tells a complex story of grief in just three lines:

The Sudden Chillness

The piercing chill I feel:

   my dead wife's comb, in our bedroom,

      under my heel . . .

Poet William Stafford said that all poems are either stories or lists. Sometimes the list *is* the story. This poem by my student Susan Kelly lists snatches of conversation in a diner to tell a waitress's story:

Diner

bacon and over

ham and lookin at ya

hi bill hows the family

graveyard stew don't spare the butter

short stack sausage well

my wife doesn't understand me

small o j java

blt hold the mayo

corned beef heavy mustard

pick up ladies

cheeseburger all the way

chocolate malt break it & shake it

put that bell where the sun don't shine joe

steak san sit on it

grilled cheese make it walkin

he wants a divorce oh honey I'm sorry

frank & beans mac & cheese up together

chicken fry beef stew single out

whats a nice girl like you

86 the mealoaf

cup a mud bowl a red side a fries

whats good separate checks

achin feet greasy hair need a cigarette

tbone still movin

stiffed snowed blown away coming through

Your story, too, may be contained in a list of details and events. Just as in prose with its series of scenes, no explanation is required. The list says it all.

Some poems use images to tell the story in a more direct way by relating an incident. Poet Robert Longoni offers a story within a story as the speaker in the poem enters his dog's dream:

On the Road to Shu

It was just another day

until our dog, a pug

named for a Chinese poet,

licked my glasses

down the middle, leaving

a vertical half-moon

smear on both lenses.

The tree between the window

and the city street

got wavy then and twice

as interesting, inside

everything went clear,

morning sun

danced with dust

above the nightstand

revealing smudges

on the paneled closet mirror—

half of me, my

looping uncombed hair

suspended on either side.

By now Li Po was asleep

across our pillows

and miraculously

between wheezes

I entered his dream

where he was

laboring behind me

on a steep mountain path

that wandered

through one of his poems,

the narrow road to Shu.

He was brave on the trail

but his legs were short

and dust flew out

from my heels, so he

shut his swollen eyes

and when the wind

spun off a rockface

lifting his ears,

imagined himself

a butterfly in flight,

hovered for a moment,

slipped ahead

to a narrow place

where light streamed

down between peaks,

then rose up, unfolding

two gloriously etched wings.

Telling your story playfully, using a dream and identification with those who can't speak for themselves and the slip-slidey details of reality and history and fantasy, can work in prose as well as poetry. Such playfulness can lift a story like Li Po's ears into new truth.

Line Breaks and Stanzas

Emerson wrote in an 1848 journal entry: "Every poem must be made up of lines that are poems." Okay, that's a bit extreme, but the point holds all these years later: Each line does something on its own, the way each scene in prose advances the story. And in poetry, you can add an extra meaning depending on where you end the line. In prose, the line stops where the auto-return chooses, but the poet can empha-size a word or add a double meaning by breaking a line ahead of time.

Here's the opening to my poem about one of my students, a man who was killed by his lover:

> When some boys in the next grade told him what goes
> where in love, he fell down in a vacant lot and cried among
> the weeds.

Here, the line length and end are determined artificially, by the width of this page. But a poet has to think beyond the words.

The line could be divided in a logical way, breaking at natural pauses:

> When some boys in the next grade told him what goes
> where in love,
>
> he fell down in a vacant lot and cried among the weeds.

The long lines make for a very slow pace, adding weightiness before the poem is ready to bear it.

> When some boys in the next grade
>
> told him what goes where in love,
>
> he fell down in a vacant lot
>
> and cried among the weeds.

These four lines are still regular units of the sentence, but they're lighter and faster now. Still, there isn't much tension to this arrange-ment, which has the flavor of chopped prose.

> When some boys
>
> in the next grade told
>
> him what goes
>
> where in love,
>
> he fell down in a vacant lot
>
> and cried among the weeds.

Going against the natural phrasing this way lends a nervous, omi-nous feel to the sentence. And the line breaks hint at double meanings:

some boys . . . told? Oh, yeah? Told what? And to whom? Is there a secret to be tattled here? *Boys told him what goes*, as in acceptable behavior, maybe? And the words at the ends of the lines—boys, for instance—get an emphasis beyond what they would if the line broke at the expected place.

How can you tell where to break lines? First, go by instinct. Second, experiment. Third, once you find some breaks that astound you with the implications they introduce into the poem, pay attention to the length of those lines and try for some consistency. Often, the eye prefers lines of equal length, and a mixture of long and short lines may lend a bumpy, uneven feel.

The poem may need to be divided into stanzas, with that powerful white space between them. Stanzas can be a trellis to support the sweet-pea vines of the lines climbing it. A uniform stanza length sometimes helps the poem's stability, and as with lines, the regular latticework can be aesthetically pleasing.

Run-on lines—enjambment—instead of end-stopped lines that are divided into "normal" units of thought can run over the white space between stanzas, too. Whether sentence units stop at the ends of stanzas or run over, it's a poetic high to leap over that white space, no explanations filling it in.

Even if you're planning to tell your story as prose, it's worth playing with poetry. Paying attention to poetry's line breaks and stanza breaks will heighten your awareness of the effects and the power of the unsaid.

Rhyme and Rhythm

Stories may have originally been set to rhyme because the reciting storytellers could remember them more easily. But, then and now, rhyme simply pleases the human ear. (I can't say about other species, but I doubt most canines notice rhyme, given their distinctly different reactions to "No" and "Go.") Rhyme and the rhythm with it can make lines that are like driftwood or a smooth shell, something not human-made but perfectly natural, sand- and water-polished. What lines do you carry with you, perhaps parts of poems you read or memorized long ago? I bet most of them rhyme.

> Tyger! Tyger! Burning bright
>
> In the forests of the night,

What immortal hand or eye

Could frame thy fearful symmetry?

> —from "The Tyger," William Blake

How many loved your moments of glad grace,

And loved your beauty with love false or true,

But one man loved the pilgrim soul in you,

And loved the sorrows of your changing face;

> —from "When You Are Old," W.B. Yeats

The grave's a fine and private place,

But none I think do there embrace.

> —from "To His Coy Mistress," Andrew Marvell

We have lingered in the chambers of the sea

By sea-girls wreathed with seaweed red and brown

Till human voices wake us, and we drown.

> —from "The Love Song of J. Alfred Prufrock," T.S. Eliot

What are the perfect lines that you return to, in your times of need? They've stayed with you because of their meanings, certainly, but it's their *sound* that makes them indelible.

Not all poems have regular patterns of rhyme (like the end rhymes above) or rhythm (like the trochaic beat of those tygers). And contemporary writers, even when they're shaping their poems into traditional forms such as sonnets, are more likely to go for the quieter effects of internal and near rhyme, and of natural rhythmic cadences. Sound still matters. But heavy-handed rhyme (spoon/moon, life/strife) and lock-step rhythm actually distract from the poem's meaning rather than help make it memorable.

How can you tell when things are working? Read aloud. You'll catch awkward moments. (I didn't see a problem with a line in a poem of mine that included "the thesaurus" until I tried to utter it.) And you'll hear when the phrasing is working too hard to make things conform—a labored reversal of normal word order, say, to make a line end with a rhyming word. You'll hear when rhyme and rhythm are trying to assume command: It's undemocratic of me to say it, I know, but they exist to serve, not rule.

Once again, even if you're planning to tell your story as prose, it's worth playing with poetry. Paying attention to poetry's rhyme and rhythm will heighten your awareness of the sound of your sentences.

Form

The design of the poem also works only to convey the content. All aspects of technique are unobtrusive servants of the story and its meanings. Adam Kirsch in a *New York Times* review complained when a poet "applies rhymes and stanzas to (content) like a coat of paint." But, he said, "When poetry succeeds as art, the meter and rhyme work with the meaning to create a higher unity, so that neither sound nor sense can be altered without changing the essence of the poem. Technique becomes merely the scaffolding that falls away when the structure is complete."

How can the form of a poem help create that "higher unity"? Before we know what framework the poem needs and what scaffolding should surround the work-in-progress, we let the process discover and explore the material. In the beginning, the-thing-that-would-be-poem hardly knows what it's about and it's too soon to shove the baggy, shapeless thing into any sort of dwelling. How do we know if it belongs in a cabin or castle until we know what *it* is?

When the story begins to take shape and show us what it might want to be, which is the best we can hope for, how do we know what sort of framework to build to house it? Should it be free verse, with its freedom from set patterns of rhyme and rhythm, or some traditional form with established "rules"? What do the poets say?

"Writing free verse," said Robert Frost, "is like playing tennis with the net down."

But here's what William Carlos Williams said: "Forcing twentieth-century America into a sonnet—gosh, how I hate sonnets—is like putting a crab into a square box. You've got to cut his legs off to make him fit. When you get through, you don't have a crab anymore."

So the Battle of the Poets won't give you the answer. Here's my answer, for which you will want to shoot me: Either. Both.

Trying your hand at free verse has benefits. First, it gets rid of conventional notions of what a poem is *supposed* to look and sound like.

Its very nature works against the predictability and archaic language that can plague traditional forms. (Although, those who think free verse is modern might take a look at the Song of Solomon in the Bible.) Second, it encourages experimentation. Playing around with lines and language teaches the writer lots about the poem construction business and lets the dwelling take its own proper shape. Writers inexperienced with poetry would do well to abandon "rules."

Writers experienced with free verse would do well to return to "rules." Traditional forms challenge and stretch skills. They force very careful word choice and line breaks. Focus on shape can lead to a refinement of technique and content that might not have been reached if the poet had quit pushing, being free-form satisfied. We can experiment with forms, too, as well as with free verse, defying a tradition or inventing a variation. Forms worth investigating include the pantoum (such as Robert Pack's "Departing Words to a Son" and Linda Pastan's "Something about the Trees"), the sestina (see Julia Alvarez's "Bilingual Sestina," Peter Meinke's "Blow, Blow Thou Winter Wind," and Karen Brennan's "Winter"), the sonnet (read your Shakespeare, of course, but look at surprises such as e.e. cummings' "next to of course god America i" and the sonnet variations in Rita Dove's book *Mother Love*), and the villanelle (must-reads include Dylan Thomas's "Do Not Go Gentle into That Good Night" and Theodore Roethke's "The Waking"; you will love Marilyn Nelson's "Daughters, 1900").

When poet and writer Sheila Bender's son died on a ski slope, I grieved for her, and I wondered, in a poem of my own, if poetry would be permitted to assuage any of her pain.

White

for Sheila

If she writes a poem

about her son's death

it won't be by assignment

it won't take the snow

and turn it into fate

it won't make him a sparrow

it won't lift him quickly

up the mountain and follow

him skis parallel straight down

the fall line. It won't

condemn trees or rock

or excuse a weak sun.

If she writes about her son's death

the page will be black with type

knots and wedges of deranged

ink. Or it will be white

no shape or trope possible

white with the true poem

waiting under the page as the blank

countenance of the mountain

waited to assign the rock beneath

its white to this boy.

The poem fell in a free verse rush right down the page. When Bender, whose poems tended toward symmetrical, graceful free verse, at last return to poetry, she moored her words in form. Her villanelle, with the power of repetition built into it, makes a pattern out of the wilderness of grief (a garden, literally in the poem's image, and figuratively in the poem's form).

A New Theology

For Seth Bender, 1975–2000

Who has no likeness of a body and has no body

is my son, now five months dead

but in my dreams, my dreams he brings the peace in
gardens,

and I see him in his smile and he is hardy

in the rolled up sleeves of his new shirt, well-fed

when he has no likeness of a body and has no body.

I see him next to me in conversation at a party

and I believe that he is fine because this is what he said,

because in my dreams, my dreams I sit with him in gardens.

The nights he comes, the cats moan long and sorry,

I believe they see his spirit entering my head,

he who has no likeness of a body and has no body.

In my life, accepting death comes slowly,

but the midwifery of sadness and of shock bleeds

afterbirth, dreams that bring the peace in gardens.

I know that he is far and he is here and he is holy.

Under sun, I feel the energy it takes to come away from God

who has no likeness of a body and has no body

who is in my dreams, the dreams that bring me gardens.

Playing with Form

Resurrect a poem you've written. Perhaps it's one you struggled with and put away. Underline the one line that most satisfies you. Count the syllables in that line. (The last line in Bender's poem above, for example, contains twelve syllables.) Now rewrite the poem so that every single line contains the exact same number of syllables as the underlined one. Cut yourself no slack. You'll have to eliminate words or find synonyms sometimes, and you'll have to break lines in strange places.

The final version may surprise you with its newly unexpected charge, its unexplainable intensity. Even if the final version is no more satisfying to you than the original, the exercise will teach you much about pushing the manipulation of lines and language, and these do-it-yourself lessons will apply to writing both traditional forms and free verse.

At a writers' conference, Marilyn Nelson told her master poets that the more restrictions they give themselves, the freer they are, allowing the surprises to show up.

Leaps and Surprises

Many readers dislike poetry because it makes them nervous and angry. They sweat, afraid they won't understand a poem, and they get mad, feeling stupid when they don't. They complain: "Why can't those people just come out and say what they mean in plain English?"

The special medium of poetry offers challenges to both reader and writer. Visibility here is different. Images are sharply delineated without all the scenic details of prose, and they're distorted, if only because they're separated from their surroundings. Colors and light are different here, and things aren't always what they appear. This is a medium with fluidity, so that images tangle and flow into each other, and with strata, so that images are layered one after another.

Readers and writers of poems put on poetry's face mask with its magic airspace, allowing views into special worlds. They let the current take them. They look not for explanations but for wonder. They seek not comprehension but a look at complexities that are unspeakable.

Given all that, poetry should make us a little nervous, I suppose.

But poems can make moves from image to image, from layer to layer, and take readers along for the ride. Poems can be accessible and subtle simultaneously. What's the story here? Who's who, what's what, what happened then? That's spoken on the page. What are the connections? What did the story mean in the narrator's life? That's underneath the page, unspoken.

At the Atlantic Center for the Arts years ago, poet James Dickey, primitive artist Howard Finster, and country singer/songwriter Janette Carter led the poets in their midst to wonder about the meaning of simplicity. Finster, whose work has been exhibited at the Smithsonian Institution's National Museum of American Art, among other places, was repairing bicycles when he received a vision from God telling him to paint. About the album covers he designed, about his "scrap art," he told his art students, "Everything that comes to me is a vision from another world." Carter, of the original Carter Family, told her music students, "Old people used to claim the fiddle was an instrument of the devil, but my daddy got him a fiddle somehow," and she shyly mentioned a New York reviewer who said she had a voice like a "hewed-out log." She was presented the National Endowment for the Arts Bess Lomax Hawes award in honor of work to preserve the old folk and country music of the Appalachians. Dickey, author of *Deliverance* and other novels and more than thirty volumes of poetry and criticism, shared the joy of the folk artists: "I'm an obsessive writer. I love words. It's like making love or dancing."

The artists and the musicians at the Center were joyfully painting and playing away with their mentors, but the poets were agonizing. What is the nature of art? What has formal education to do with it? Where does it come from? Tell us about simplicity, we students demanded. Where does art come from? What about training—painting on bicycles, touring as an autoharp player at twelve, winning the National Book Award?

I was trying to figure myself out as a writer. What did I dare write about? What about personal material as opposed to invention? What was my voice? What about style? What forms should I learn and practice? What about editors' views and publication? There are times when a writer is especially open and vulnerable—and usually meets the right people at those right times. Back then, I needed answers.

So I was ripe to hear James Dickey's answer about simplicity in art. "Be simple," he said, "but in an astonishing way." It was precisely what I needed to hear—and have never forgotten.

Stories can be accessible, events and situations understood on a first reading. That's simplicity. (If there were no more to the story, it would be simplistic.) Then those same stories, twined with other stories, turn complex. "Simple" art gives the surface story and also yields the unspoken story.

It accomplishes this with technique so graceful that it's invisible. Van Gogh understood: "Let us try to master the mysteries of technique to such an extent that people are deceived by it and will swear by all that is holy that we have *no* technique. Let our work be so savant that it seems naïve and does not stink of our sapience . . ." A high compliment for anything well done is always, "You make it look so easy."

In writing your story—fiction, nonfiction, poetry, whatever—be simple, yes. But in an astonishing way.

Making Leaps

A significant element of simplicity is silence. Part of the craft of story-telling is knowing when to shut up. Stanza breaks in poems and section breaks in prose can be more evocative than half a dictionary's worth of words.

A collage story places fragments and pieces side by side with no explanation or even obvious connection. It simply cuts from scene to scene. Writing an essay, a short story, or a poem in collage style is ter-rific practice in making leaps. Here is an exercise to illustrate this point.

1. First, choose a category. It should be something specific: not love or beauty, for instance, but kisses or dogs. Nancy Mairs' mem-oir *Remembering the Bone House: An Erotics of Space and Place* uses the category of houses, focusing each chapter on a house in which she once lived, with chapter titles including "In Exeter" and "The Farm." The category could be ages. Poet Tom Speer wrote "The Poet as a Boy" with different sections of the poem launched with "At eight," "At twelve," and "At fifteen." Besides "Beds," two pieces of which follow, writer Cheryl Diane Kidder has written stories titled "Dresses" and "Cars."

2. Write a series of scenes, each one a snapshot focusing tightly on a different experience with the chosen category. Start each one with a subtitle.

The pieces can be set down one after the other in chronological order, or they can be juxtaposed in a cut-up order. They are merely placed beside each other with nothing but a break of white space between them.

Look at this section from Kidder's "Beds" as an example:

1987, San Francisco

Called in sick at work for a week straight when I first met Tony. Every day waking up in my green geometric-pat-terned southwest sheets, the skin on his palms darker than my nipples. Three mornings, pure fog out the lace curtains. I'd turn over against his back and close my eyes, only him between me and the light.

If we woke up again he'd pull the sheet over his back, smil-ing down on me and come in without knocking. No was never a possibility. My head bent back over the edge of the mattress, upside down rocking pictures on my nightstand, then dark, then the ceiling, cracked from recent tremors, then dark. Never wanted to leave the apartment then. We'd bring the dishes, a big tub of butter and just-popped toast over, eat for a while, push the dishes off onto the floor and climb under the sheets again.

If I'd had a Spanish-English dictionary we would have never left, but finally we wanted to say things to each other beyond those that could be signed. I bought a pocket Merriam-Webster's and bent back the cover. These pages were dog-eared: enamorado, empezar, linda, guapo, para siempre.

1973, San Jose

Comfortably worn cotton sheets on a double-wide futon the morning after my third or fourth frat party. Rick had a huge head of dark hair, curly, like his moustache, and a New York accent. He'd just been through est and we'd talked about it for hours. I wanted to get rid of this virginity curse and had made a decision. Wine glasses on turned-over wooden crates, a couple of beaded necklaces, an ashtray half-full of his cigarettes and a roach clip. Bedspread batiked and flimsy that got caught up between my legs.

He taught philosophy and was fourteen years older. The bedroom's wood floor was full of cardboard boxes. Maybe he'd be moving in, maybe away, depending. He was up early for an early class. I took longer, though—his place was always so cold. I shuffled along the wood floor, collecting my things, turned the old glass door handle to go, smelled the incense we'd burned the night before.

"Beds" portrays a woman whose life has no center. There is life outside the bed, for she buys clothes, goes to work, and has a child, but these aspects are background to the bed's foreground. Her recording, as if in a journal, of her compulsive behavior suggests that she's looking closely at the details in order to see the pattern. The nonchronological montage shows her jumbled attempt to understand herself. The story's elliptical, fragmented style works very well to reveal her, directly and indirectly, to the reader. Understanding happens between the lines and in the white space. By the end of the final snapshot, the reader knows, along with the narrator, that beds aren't the doors into love, that she will never find that door.

Besides more conventionally structured stories, Kidder has published other collage-type stories, two of which have been nominated for the Pushcart Prize. But, she says, "'Beds' was the first time I used my notion of how we remember things to drive the structure of a story. I started out by telling myself I was just making an outline of stories I wanted to write in the future. Each section started out with a specific date, but the dates were not exactly chronological. I wanted to explore the weight of the space in between the sections."

Leaping into the abyss—seeking and speaking truths—takes courage. Taking leaps between scenes in stories requires a different kind of courage: to keep silent. Sometimes truth can't be spoken out loud and can only be seen, below us, as we make an exhilarating flying leap over white space.

8

LISTENING TO THE CRITICS:
DEALING WITH READERS

Okay. You've passed Courage 101. You're committed to looking closely at your experiences and telling your stories honestly. Your report card says you are brave enough to take these risks, even when it means running with scissors.

You are ready for Courage 102. It takes courage, too, to show your stories.

One talented writer I know froze up for two years after an author at a writers' conference had a strong negative reaction to his story's content. An editor, who was trying her hand at fiction of her own, told another writer that a detail about cactus blooming was inaccurate. That writer told me, "I couldn't write after that. I wanted to take that bitch up to my house in September and shove her face in the fall blooms." Another writer stopped showing her poems when a classmate wrote "This sucks" in the margin.

Even well-intended suggestions for improving a story can inhibit writers.

Yet we need an audience and we need others' reactions. If Mom and your writers' group say, "Your story made me cry. It's brilliant, don't change a word," you can bask for a few minutes in the glowing words but then you're going to want more than abstract praise. Sign up for Courage 102 and learn who your best critics are, what kind of feedback is most useful, and how to use criticism. There's extra credit for playing well with others.

Who Are Your Best Critics?

The most important people in our lives, those whose admiration and praise we most hope for, are usually our least useful critics. They lack objectivity. They love us and don't want to hurt our feelings. And if they're not writers themselves, they may not know how to offer more than "I like it, honey" or "Something doesn't seem right about this."

Taking a class or joining a writers' group may provide the encouragement and feedback your writing needs to advance. Formal writers' workshops and classes, along with less structured writers' groups, may differ in individual practices, but they share benefits and hazards enough to be nearly synonymous. Choose carefully, and if it becomes apparent that the workshop was the wrong choice, move on.

Workshops have advantages in addition to providing an intelligent audience. Participation helps us learn how to listen to criticism and how to deal with it. We learn what to aspire to as critics ourselves. We learn how to articulate the reasons for our reactions to stories. In analyzing others' stories, we learn how to apply the same critical eye to our own work.

What qualities should you look for in a workshop, whether a class or writers' group?

Choose a group whose members are working on your level and higher. You are not in competition, of course, but working with less experienced beginners can be frustrating because they may not have developed critical agility yet. You may want to *teach* them how to critique (and how to write), an inclination that won't endear you to the workshop leader or the other members (trust me on this) and works against your purpose for joining in the first place. Instead, you'll rise with the group's tide when you work with those sharing or exceeding your level of skill and experience.

Join a group that has some ground rules. Ask what they are, or, with a new group, discuss what rules might be invented. Here are suggestions to make the workshop a safe place to take the risks of writing and showing your bold, honest work:

- Agree that writing shown to the group is for their eyes only. When members want to show a story to an outsider, they ask permission.

- My "don't ask, don't tell" policy helps the group focus on the story itself rather than on the writer's personal life. Practice of this policy means that no one in the group is allowed to ask the writer about the story's origins in personal experience, nor is the writer allowed to explain how the story grew out of real-life events.

- Avoid the word "you" in talking about the character or speaker in the story. "Why did you kill your husband on page five"?

or "You must have really hated your mother" assume that the writer and the story's character or voice are the same. Even when they essentially are the same, as in memoir, personal essay, and often poetry, the persona on the page isn't identical to the writer and can never be identical given the selective nature of storytelling, the ways real experiences are shaped for the page, and the writer's subjectivity.

- I recommend that the writer whose story is being discussed keep silent. This practice helps the writer listen open-mindedly to comments rather than rush in to explain or disagree. At the end, the writer can be ungagged and should use the time not to defend or justify aspects of the story, but to ask questions and seek clarification.

- Agree to forget personal and political agendas when discussing stories. The group's role is not to stamp its approval (or rejection) onto a story but to analyze it. In stories, people will not always behave well (and that's a good thing, too, for how dull they would be without conflict); they'll utter expletives (yes, including the F word). The writer doesn't set out to shock or offend, of course, but to find the truth, offering the details and language to show that truth. Autopsies will be performed and living wounds opened, and you need writers who don't faint at the sight of blood. Writer Kingsley Amis said, "If you can't annoy someone, there's little point in writing."

All the writers I know, whether they've been in writers' groups or not, have at least a couple of trusted readers whose comments help them think out problems in the story and revise. Such readers are worth finding and honoring.

How to Play Critic

The notion of offering and receiving "criticism" makes some writers nervous. It sounds so negative, as if the critics are baring their file-sharpened teeth and ripping into the story's tender flesh. Substituting "criticism" with "analysis, interpretation, and suggestions" may help. Whatever we call it, we are not talking about judgment. The most useful feedback first examines the nature and intentions of the story and then discusses what helps the story live up to itself and what works against it—and why.

Dos

Responding to others' writing will improve your own writing. I guarantee it. Your thoughtful comments will benefit the other writers (and will encourage the same level of commentary when they read your stories), but more than anything, as you analyze the effects achieved by different approaches and techniques, as you force yourself to articulate the reasons for your reactions (negative or positive), you'll teach yourself more than a dozen good books on writing ever could. Poet Donald Justice pointed out that "criticism can be of enormous value in helping to define and refine one's own thinking; and there is always the chance, if the criticism is any good, that it might do the same for others."

What kinds of comments are helpful for both you and the other writers?

When we read a story in manuscript form, we tend to jump straight into critique mode, pen primed to fill up margins, editing option turned on. As in some arguments or discussions, when each party is preparing the next remark instead of listening to what the other is saying, sometimes readers are so busy thinking of the comments they should be making that they're hardly reading the story itself. And the very setup seems to demand that the reviewer find something wrong with the manuscript. I regularly see this disappointed comment: "I'm sorry, I wish I had suggestions for improvement, but your story's perfect as it is."

It's a good idea to read a story first just as you would if it were published, giving it the benefit of the doubt, assuming all will be explained and fulfilled by the end.

Then, before making any notes on the pages, begin your comments with a sentence or paragraph describing what the story is about—the material it's exploring (its themes, if you will, as opposed to its events). This approach takes practice but is worth cultivating. First, it benefits the writers, who sometimes see that others didn't read the story they'd meant to write or who may see enough variety in readers' descriptions to realize the story lacks focus. Insightful readers will also be able to point out the significance of certain details, repetitions, and connections written in subconsciously and not yet fully realized.

Second, the description of what the story is about helps readers to see a story's intentions, analyze it, and talk about it in its own terms. Actually writing (rather than speaking) the description lets the discovery process work for comments on others' writing, just as it does in story writing. Your own insights will surprise you.

With the story's own intentions in mind, reviewers can look at the ways the story's shape and techniques help or hinder its becoming the story it wants to be, not the story reviewers think it should be or the story *they* would have written.

Here's a model by writer Shannon Cain, who provided a set of comments on fellow workshopper Rachael Cupp's "White Coats and Halos" that can illustrate the approach even though you haven't seen the story she's critiquing:

> This story explores the effects on a young woman of discovering the aftermath of a horrifically violent fatality involving family members. She is haunted by guilt, blaming herself somehow because she told her sister she should marry the man who eventually murdered her and her infant son. Her guilt and pain are brought to the fore with her neighbor's cruelty regarding the pigeons. As with her sister, she blames herself for their deaths since she fed them and they continue to flock to the place where he runs them down with his car.

> I absolutely loved how you detailed this woman's mental illness—the sounds she hears when she shakes her head; falling asleep on the dirty rug with one shoe; the laughter of the downtown people in the restaurant; the overly bright outdoors. Her surroundings are so intrusive and scary that I can practically hear all the noises in her head. This is a very auditory story. The sounds are almost another character—pigeon bones, cracking glass. Come to think of it, the visual and tactile details are wonderful, too. Formica, hot water. Pigeon parts in rubber-gloved hands? What an image. Washing her hands repeatedly, and washing clean dishes: details like that let us know she's crazy, without a huge dramatic scene or clichéd madwoman stuff.

> The character is struggling so hard to hold on to herself. It is unbearably sad that she loses this struggle at the end, and ironic that her mental condition, perhaps brought on by the trauma she had, ends up in bloody violence at her own hand as well.

Note how the critic opens with a paragraph interpreting the story's events (not merely recounting them). Note how the positive comments are specific, beyond "I love the details" or "good job of showing state of mind," to include examples, the meaning of the examples, and the connections implied in the story.

Here's another analytical sample:

> "Down" is the story of a boy trapped in a shifting, vertiginous world where things are always in motion, dizzy, and cold. After a terrible experience, when he almost drowns and his little sister does drown, he exists in a world where "everything falls." Gravity and the bottom of the lake and the grave pull everything down. But the vision of his sister is in a world of up. The surreal details work so very well to capture—no, to create—this boy's world as his parents and Dr. Young ("old" Dr. Young!) try to help him come back to the normal world of equilibrium. And finally, when he re-experiences the drowning—in an intense rushing drowning of a long sentence—he understands that his sister is never going to return. At the end, he understands that it is her forgiveness he needs, and in understanding that, the world is level for him again.

Marginalia

In addition to comments such as Cain's, notes on the manuscript's pages and at the end, upon a second or third reading, can help the writer revise. Since the reviewer's role is not to edit or rewrite, what kinds of notes are useful?

- Point out inconsistencies (Gertie was a blonde back on page five) and dubious word choices and factual errors (no armadillos in Phoenix). Any writers' group has vast and encyclopedic knowledge—one member knows guns, another the subways of New York City, another diseases of dogs, another court procedures—which is a wonderful resource. A warning, though: Don't let detail distract your focus on the story's explorations and intentions.

- Talk about the story's design and structure: beginnings, the order of scenes, pacing, endings. Does the story begin at the right place? Are all scenes necessary? Where is the greatest tension? Are there flat or saggy stretches in the story, where nothing much is advanced or revealed? Does the story end at the right place? Are there too many flashbacks? Are scenes presented in the most effective order, whether chronological or not?

- Talk about the people in the story. What are the main folks, including the narrator, like? What motivates them? What are their conflicts? What are their relationships with each other? What brings them to life? Are minor players distractingly over-developed? Does the narrator's voice come through? Are major players sufficiently developed?

- Discuss the style: wordiness, density, sparseness, economy of language, use of figurative language, rhythm. Do tone and language suit the story? Detract from it? Enhance it? In what ways and why?

- Before declaring that some aspect of the story doesn't work, first consider why the writer might have made such a choice. Write about that before concluding whether or not you think it works.

  Before writing or uttering the classic workshop phrase, "I would like to see more of . . ." again consider *why* the writer might have included *less* of it. If you conclude at last that more would help the story go deeper or take the reader more fully into the story, explain your reasons. And if you can find another way of phrasing it, bless you.

- Here's a suggestion about which I'm a bit fanatical. Okay, all right. I guess one can't be just sort of fanatical, so I'll go all the way here: no crossing out. It is out of bounds to draw a line through, make the delete squiggle upon, or cross out even a single word that someone else has set on the page. The reviewer's job is to ask questions and point out concerns and make suggestions. It is not to edit or rewrite. It's okay to write in a correct spelling, if you are so inclined, though the teacher in me says it's better just to mark the spelling error (sp?) and let the writer correct it. It is out of bounds to "improve" another's writing by "fixing" it or even, heaven forbid, deleting it. Sometimes the reviewer will, for example, have a great idea for the right ending and it takes a strong will to resist the temptation to offer this wonderful gift to the writer. But it is a far better thing to talk about why the present ending doesn't satisfy and to ask questions. The new ending that the writer comes up with is bound to be truer to the story than anything even the most brilliant reviewer could impose. It is the ultimate disrespect to cross out. Okay, okay, I'm a fanatic on the subject.

- Each reviewer develops a system for marking a manuscript. It's no surprise that I prefer putting pencil to pages on my desk to making screen notes. After all, I am not editing. I underline words and lines that I find particularly effective. A really fine paragraph gets a big plus sign. Often, in the margin, I tell the writer why. I use a squiggly underline beneath a questionable word or phrase, and in the margin I tell the writer why. I put parentheses around words, phrases, or sentences (sometimes entire paragraphs) that I think the writer might consider omitting. (Parentheses are a gentle way of avoiding crossing out. They allow the writer to choose.) Other reviewers might use different-colored highlighters. If you're making page notes, make sure to provide the key to the system so the writer knows how to interpret it.

- In the margin, I ask questions about the people and credibility: *I wonder why . . . ? Why would Clarissa believe . . . ? What's Phillip's motivation here?* I ask questions about technique: *Might this be the real beginning? Should this flashback appear later, once the story's in full motion?* You get the idea. Questions allow the writer to consider and choose and finally, to be true to the story.

All of these considerations are analytical, not judgmental. They show respect for the story by looking at it in its own terms, and they show respect for the writer by looking at the story objectively, separating the writer from the writing.

Don'ts

- Resist the temptation to be clever. Funny comments are rarely humorous to the writer whose story is under review. At worst, they're disguised cheap shots. At best, they're about the reviewer showing off rather than giving the story writer the respect of careful attention.

- Some comments are not only useless but harmful. An example, which I wish weren't true: "This story made no sense whatsoever to me. I have no idea what this story is actually about.

I believe that this writer is capable of writing something worthwhile. This story, however, is not it. The fragmented, confused nature of the story (dare I mention spelling and grammar errors?) makes the very capable writer of this story come off as amateur and unskilled."

- Other comments aren't so blatantly less-than-useful:

   1. "I don't like this kind of story." "I've read too many incest stories." "I hate science fiction." It's helpful for the readers to acknowledge if they aren't well read in a certain area or aren't familiar with a genre's conventions, but dismissing a story because of the subject or genre helps neither writer nor reader.

   2. "I don't like the narrator." Worrying about the likability of the people in stories tames them into a niceness, a blandness to which no one can object. The question readers should ask is not, "Would I want to be friends with the narrator?" but "Is the narrator convincing?"

   3. "The language is offensive." Editors of Norman Mailer's World War II novel *The Naked and the Dead* worried that readers would be offended by the soldiers' rough language and substituted words such as "fuggin'." When the book appeared, Mary McCarthy sent a telegram: "Great book, Norman, but you should learn how to spell 'fuck.'" That little anecdote may be apocryphal, but if it isn't true, it should be.

   4. The key: Is the language true to the speaker? That is the only consideration.

   5. "I can identify with this." Not bad to hear, but not helpful, either. The fact that a reader has had a similar experience indicates nothing about the story's effectiveness. And though I enjoy well-written stories that touch on my history, I truly relish stories that take me into worlds I don't know.

   6. "I really enjoyed this." "Good story." Okay, thanks. And . . . and . . . ?

   7. "If this were my story, I would . . ." But it's not, so don't.

   8. Then there's the comment that's trying really hard to find something positive to say: "I like your choice of font."

Workshop Hazards

We write in solitude, going vulnerable and unprotected into the dark alone. We emerge with pages in hand, and it's then we want and need to offer them to readers. Now it's time—*after* the labor—to put on the protective helmet.

How do we use readers' commentary?

Remember that the purpose here is not heavenly praise but earthly guidance. You sought good readers' comments not to participate in a mutual admiration society but to read each other's work with respect, that is to say with honesty.

When your story is being discussed and you aren't allowed to speak, stay loose. Jot down notes for follow-up questions. Listen open-mindedly. Just maybe some of your readers know what they're talking about. Yes, they're pointing out the defects in your creation, your precious child, and yes, only you are really allowed to criticize your own. But listen, just listen.

When it's your turn to speak, don't waste time trying to explain or defend. Just ask questions to make sure you understand the comments. Use the time to ask additional questions about aspects of the story you yourself wondered about, things that weren't brought up in the discussion.

Some writers hurry to read everyone's comments immediately after the workshop. Some wait until the next day. Some listen to the discussion and then read individuals' comments only weeks later, when they're ready to revise. Different strokes and all that. I recommend that the ones who look at the comments before the discussion has cooled put them away for a few days before looking at them again. The comments that seemed harsh and stupid-headed will be gentler and more thoughtful in the clearer light cast by a little distance.

So: Resist the temptation to send a group email to your fellow work-shoppers along these lines: "Going over the critiques from last night, I thought I would address a few things . . . A couple of people pinged the adjectives in the dialogue . . . I also had a ping about the use of the characters' names in the dialogue . . . Some of you disliked . . ." with every objection followed by a lengthy defense.

Give it time. And then resist the temptation anyway.

The comments that most bother you, that most upset you, that most anger you may—I'm sorry—be the ones to pay closest attention to. Some comments should be dismissed as thoughtless and agenda-directed, yes, but it's often true that the most upsetting comments disturb us because we know at heart they're right. *Damn, I thought I could get away with that*. But no. The criticism that feels awful may be what's most worth paying attention to.

At the same time, not everything that feels awful is useful or right. The key is to be honest with yourself and to be true to your story.

Never allow anyone to rewrite for you. Forget the authority of those eager to rewrite, whether they're your teachers or your respected fellow writers, and remember that the story is *yours*. Give thoughtful consideration to suggestions, but finally, be true to your own story.

Don't try to accommodate all readers' suggestions in your revision. I've seen many a lively story, whatever its flaws, tamed into blandness when it attempts to answer every reader's every objection and to accommodate every reader's every suggestion. The result is a bowl of tepid pudding nobody could object to. It has no flavor or texture whatsoever and nobody wants to eat it, either.

There will be those who cross out your words, despite my workshop protocol. You can either throw out their comments altogether or pretend there are parentheses around questionable passages rather than crossings-out and think about them. You know what you need to do. Consider comments honestly. Then make up your own mind. This is your story. Nobody else knows its intricacies, its nuances, its truths. Tell them. Listen to see where they're not coming through. Revise accordingly. But be true to your story. That's all there is to it.

Hard Hat Zone

As useful as workshops can be, there are dangers, some blatant and some insidious. Writers who are aware of the dangers may be able to protect themselves. Put on your hard hat against these hazards:

- Everybody in the first writers' group I joined was writing science fiction. So the stories I wrote to show the group were SF, which, in my case, stood for Stinky Failure. It's hazardous to the health of the writer to write for someone else's expectations.

- When I risked showing the science-fiction group a mainstream piece, their other-worldly taste for the bizarre found my story tediously down-to-earth. Whether the story worked or not, the group wasn't the right audience for it and couldn't offer useful comments. Having a story measured against others' set standards rather than viewed in its own light can be demoralizing.

- Writing for a particular group can inhibit the writer's growth. Writing for *any* group has its hazards. Awareness that we're going to show a story to our group can make us play it safe rather than take risks. The nature of workshops, even the best ones, can lead to a flattening out of individuality. Writers in university writing programs are even more vulnerable than those participating in less formal groups. Joy, a student of mine who wrote delightfully quirky, odd, and surprising little poems, paid me a visit after a year in an MFA program. The new poems she showed me were polished and (perhaps) more technically skillful, but they were clones of poems I see in many workshops and journals. They'd lost the strange and special Joyness of the earlier work. In her novel *Range of Light*, Valerie Miner wrote: "The academy processed your mind the way Kraft processed cheese, removing the impurities and idiosyncrasies and originality."

    Writers' groups and programs are useful and valuable in many ways. Awareness of potential influences can help writers protect their individuality while claiming the benefits.

    Heed poet Carolyn Kizer's words about her experience in a class taught by Theodore Roethke: " . . . the most important thing Roethke ever said to me was after class when another student was very critical of some eccentric thing I had done, and Ted admonished him, 'You want to be very careful when you criticize something like that, because it may be the hallmark of an emerging style.' He knew that our eccentricities are part of our true voice."

- Sometimes writers "workshop" a story to death. They tweak it endlessly, sending it by the group with each tweaking, until it begins to spoil and the group can't respond with any freshness. An overworked story lacks crispness at best and turns rotten at worst.

- Some writers turn into workshop junkies, forever joining yet another group and, often, recycling the same few stories rather than going forward to create new stories. Participating in the group offers the illusion that writing is happening when in fact it's a substitute for writing.

- A writing group can boost you up when you're down, discouraged, doubtful. Others in the group have been there, too. Go ahead and commiserate and accept commiseration. For five minutes. Then turn to the writing at hand.

- Writers' groups and workshops can be therapeutic. The therapy comes, for both writer and reader, from the exploration of the material and the shaping of the material. The writing group needs to guard against becoming a support group for behavioral, emotional, and mental health issues. Excellent virtual and face-to-face support groups can provide coping strategies and community. The writers' group is about the writing. And the group's focus is not on diaries and journals but on the crafted and artful story at hand.

- We never outgrow the need for feedback from trusted readers. Eventually, the time spent in writers' groups may have diminishing returns. The group can offer security, but sometimes the writer needs to disarm the alarm system and invite all manner of strangers in. The group can be a safe haven, but what the writer really needs is to go unprotected and alone into the storm.

Meg's House Rules

Here's my manifesto for workshop protocol, behavior, and attitude. Feel free to steal it.

1. We respect the act of writing. We honor the impulse and the attempt to write. We will not discourage writing with cheap shots or nonconstructive comments.

2. We respect the stories themselves. We show that respect by taking them seriously. We read each story in its own terms. We read carefully, appreciating subtlety and originality. We do not judge. Judgment is not the group's function. We don't dismiss a story because of its subject matter or style or genre; we attempt to understand it. We consider a story's intentions and then analyze it to suggest how and where and why its design and other technical aspects help it accomplish its intentions.

3. We respect the writer. We remember that it takes courage to expose stories. We are not in competition with each other. We honor individuality, for voice and our separate, wonderfully strange approaches are at the heart of fresh, lively writing. We will always keep a clear distinction between the speaker in the story and the writer. We will check at the door our opinions on politics, religion, lifestyle, and the superiority of cats over dogs.

4. We respect our readers. We suppress defensiveness and listen open-mindedly to suggestions and analyses. We understand that readers are as individual as writers, that not every reader will respond to or comprehend our stories in the same ways.

5. We respect ourselves. Though we suffer doubts, minor or grave, if it is in us to write, we will continue to write. A *New York Times Book Review* article reminded us that "The one article of faith that unites all successful writers, however diverse their work and temperaments, is the necessity of inextinguishable belief in oneself."

When Workshops Go Bad

Norman Stock, in his collection *Buying Breakfast for My Kamikaze Pilot*, offers an example:

Thank You for the Helpful Comments

I sit quietly listening

as they tear my poem to shreds in the poetry workshop

as each one says they have a "problem" with this line

and they have a "problem" with that line

and I am not allowed to speak because that is the

etiquette of the workshop

so I sit listening and writhing while they tear the guts out

of my poem and leave it lying bleeding and dead

and when they're finally finished having kicked the

stuffing out of it

having trimmed it down from twenty lines to about four

words that nobody objects to

then they turn to me politely and they say well Norman

do you have any response

response I say picking myself up off the floor and brushing

away the dirt while holding on for dear life to what I

thought was my immortal poem now dwindled to nothing

and though what I really want to say is can I get my money

back for this stupid workshop what I say instead is . . .

uh . . . thank you for your helpful comments . . .

while I mumble under my breath motherfuckers

wait till I get to *your* poems

Back to the Workshop

When you return to your writers' group, remember how it feels to be on the receiving end of thoughtless, pompous, or harsh comments. Practice explaining your reactions to others' stories and the reasons for your reactions in your own words. Honesty plus tact equals respect.

The next chapter will guide you in using criticism of your stories as you revise them.

For now, finally, no matter what others say and no matter how you doubt, keep the faith. Write, simply write. That's all.

9

KNOWING WHAT'S TRUE:
REVISING STORIES

You've been invited to a party. You're not totally sure you belong, but you're eager to join anyway. Maybe you wangled your own invitation. You shower, you dress in the new exotic thing you know looks really hot. It's a good hair day.

You get lost trying to find the party house. You curse, you sweat. Finally, you find the street, park, and knock on the door. You introduce yourself to the person who opens the door and get a puzzled look. Oops. Wrong house. You're ready to give up, just go home and sit alone in your finery, watch a movie and eat cookie-dough ice cream straight out of the carton. You didn't belong at that party anyway.

Then you spot the sign stuck in the lawn of the house across the street. PARTY HERE. You're nervous. Maybe nobody will talk to you, and what if they're all watching amateur dance videos on YouTube. But you square your shoulders and enter.

And the party's great. Once you're inside the right place, you loosen up, laugh, meet funny new people, you do the limbo before the night's over (yes, the limbo), and the salsa you spill on yourself doesn't show too badly on your exotic duds. When one host says to the other (as my in-laws used to), "Honey, let's go to bed, these folks might want to go home," you can't believe three hours have flown by.

Back home, you collapse. You're beat. You sleep the happy sleep of the fulfilled. In the morning, you wake and wonder why you feel a glow, and then you recall, oh yes, you went to that great party, and everybody loved you.

After a couple cups of coffee, you begin to replay things. You hear your too-hearty laugh at a lame joke. You must have looked a fool trying to dance horizontal under a broomstick. In daylight, the salsa stain really really shows.

You're up, you're down. A friend calls and agrees it was one terrific party, and all you can think is whether you'll ever be invited to another one.

You're suffering post-party anxiety.

And this is the way it goes with writing, too. Do I really belong in the company of writers? you wonder. You prepare yourself as best you can, learning the craft, sharpening your pencils. You flounder with each new piece, unable to find your way in. What made you think you could ever write, anyway? Then suddenly, without awareness, you're in the story's stride, oblivious to all else. You're in the world of the story, not thinking about whether the writing is good or bad. When you finally come to, you are wonderfully exhausted. The next day, you look at your pages. Where did this come from? you wonder. Did I write this? Wow.

Hours later you take another look. The story is stupid, the sentences and the language are terrible. The pages stink on ice. You hide them away in despair.

Still, you can't help yourself: Later you bring them out again. And darned if they aren't pretty good this time. But no doubt you've run the well dry, and it'll never fill up again.

You're suffering post-writing anxiety.

Maybe it helps to know you're not alone. Maybe it helps to understand the pattern and to know that doubt is, for most of us, always part of it. Then you can remind yourself that your role is to write and then to revise what you've written, not to judge it. Instead of labeling it wonderful or horrible, brilliant, or hopeless, remember Grace Paley's words: Not good or bad but true or false.

The Purpose of Drafts

It's tempting after a first draft to run a spellcheck, tinker with a word or three, save the document, and call it done.

Exciting surprises and discoveries have happened in the first draft. Some are true to the story and some are false. Some belong and some should be shelved for the next story. Some need to be connected or brought closer to the surface and some are misleading tangents. Time now for the next draft.

Bernard Malamud said that he wrote a story three times, at least: "Once to understand it, the second time to improve the prose, and a third to compel it to say what it still must say."

Here's a first draft of a poem by Tom Speer, a member of my poetry writers' group:

Fear of Choking

In the dream

a small man

lifts me, weightless,

on his shoulder

and carries me out

my bedroom window.

I am wearing purple socks

and white pajamas,

and holding a piece of bread.

Night after night

I wake to this dream,

to this man with small hands,

rough beard, and deep, soft eyes.

Awaken

so utterly frightened

I cannot scream. My fear

is caught in my throat.

I swallow it whole

like a bird

and waken

to the flapping of wings.

Well, the group said, what's this poem about? We picked a nit (the bird metaphor at the end is mixed up) and suggested that adding more details might help the poem discover its meaning. Here's the next draft Speer brought to the group:

Dream

I remember a childhood dream,

when I was five or six,

living in Topeka, Kansas,

sleeping upstairs in an old Victorian.

That was the year the locusts

came out of pitchy trees, turned

day into night, that year I said

prayers to my guardian angel,

and I hated no one.

In the dream a man came into my room,

pulled me out of bed over his shoulder like a jacket,

a small man, with a dry beard, dark face,

dark hollows for eyes.

I hear locusts storming, the man is tapping,

lifting me down the ladder.

I am wearing purple socks and white pajamas,

holding a piece of bread,

and I look up to see my family waving from the window

goodbye boy, goodbye, they are yelling.

In the dream I am screaming back,

but no sound comes, only

a catch in the throat,

and I am hanging there

on the ladder, looking up,

hearing the caw of a black crow.

Well, it's coming along, the group told him. Some nice new details have appeared ("pitchy trees"), and the childhood references at the beginning seem suggestive. The psychologist in our group declared that other people's dreams are boring. So what's it about? we still wanted to know. The third version grew substantially:

Untitled

So in the dark classroom I am watching

the noted poet and octogenarian as he motions us

to sink down into the depths, into dream,

and he reads his poem in which he meets his

mother and father on a road, and I remember

the dream began when I was five or six,

living in Topeka, Kansas, sleeping upstairs

in an old Victorian. That was the year

the locusts came out of pitchy trees, turned

day into night, that was the year I said

prayers to my guardian angel, and hated no one.

In the dream a man came into my room,

pulled me out of bed like a jacket. He was

a small man, with a dry beard, dark face,

hollows for eyes. I hear locusts storming.

The man is tapping, lifting me down the ladder.

I am wearing purple socks and white pajamas,

holding a piece of bread, and I look up to see

my family waving from the window, goodbye boy,

goodbye boy, goodbye, they are yelling,

and I am screaming back, but no sound comes,

only a catch in the throat. I am hanging

on the ladder, looking up. I write this dream

and take it to my group on a small piece

of paper, because this is a low self-esteem

dream, and everyone says bring a microscope

next time, and anyway says my psychologist friend,

dreams are boring, so what's it mean, and why

should we read this dream, or care about it,

and I remember that was the year I stopped praying

and we moved one day to California where

it was said by the neighbors, we would suffer

earthquakes, that was the year the great tornado

came to Topeka and flattened our street,

killed our neighbors, tore the trees out of the earth,

that was the year when everything seemed different;

I looked at bread, at socks, at wood, and they

were suddenly alive, and full of meaning.

Well, oh my, will you look at that? we said. Now you're getting some-where. There's a lot of extraneous stuff in here this time, but it needed to be written in to force the discoveries at the end. The poem had to grow before it could be cut back to its essence. The poet had to ask, in writing, what the dream meant before the poem could discover it. The final revision cut away everything that didn't belong and left the details that showed the meaning of the dream and the child's initiation as he awakens, unprotected but vital, into an uncertain and unsafe world:

Dream

The dream began when I was five or six,

living in Topeka, Kansas, sleeping upstairs

in an old Victorian. That was the year

the locusts came out of pitchy trees,

turned day into night, the year I said prayers

to my guardian angel, and hated no one.

In the dream a man came into my room,

pulled me out of bed over his shoulder like a jacket,

a small man, with a dry beard, dark face,

dark hollows for eyes. Still I hear the locusts

storming, the man tapping the wooden rungs

lifting me down the ladder. I am wearing purple

socks and white pajamas and I look up to see

my family waving from the window *goodbye boy*

goodbye they are yelling and I scream back,

but no sound comes, only a catch in the throat.

That was the year I stopped praying, and we

moved one day to California where, people said,

we would suffer earthquakes, and that year

the great tornado swept through Topeka and flattened our

street, killed our neighbors, tore the trees out of the earth,

and everything resounded, and was different;

I looked at bread, at socks, at wood, and they

were suddenly alive, and full of meaning.

Your drafts often will follow this groping, expanding, contracting process. Guided by your writers' group, or especially by your own instinct and self-honesty, you can push the story, draft by draft, until it yields its truth.

From Draft to Draft

After the heat of its first draft, a story needs to cool off. Give yourself time to develop objectivity. For me, the length of time is related to the length of the story. A poem needs to be put out on the windowsill just overnight, while a short story or essay requires two days, and a book doesn't begin to set enough for objectivity until a week. There isn't a definite cooling-off period you can set your kitchen timer for; paying attention to your own habits can help you form your best personal timetable. However, don't wait *too* long, or it'll turn cold and stale.

Then read the whole draft through. You're not editing or tidying up yet but preparing to revise. At this point, revision isn't merely cosmetic but is re-envisioning, re-seeing the story. Make notes as you read, even if you're sure you'll remember what you're noticing. What problems are you seeing? What thematic threads do you see? What is the story wanting to explore?

This stage can be painful. Rewriting leads to more rewriting. As you change one thing, other things will have to be changed; you can't disturb a detail without disturbing the universe of the story. But this can also be pleasurable as you help the story find itself.

Next, read the story aloud—to yourself, to another, to your device, or to your dog, it doesn't really matter. A musician friend told me, "You start recording it and the truth comes out."

Here are main considerations in guiding the story to its truth:

1. Is a strong and convincing voice coming through?
2. What issues, conflicts, relationships, and memories has the story begun to explore (no matter what you initially intended or planned)?

True revision—re-envisioning—sometimes means putting the first draft aside and writing it again without consulting the original. If the voice is wimpy or undistinguished, no amount of tinkering will pep it up and give it authority. If the thematic threads haven't yet made it to the loom, no amount of rearranging will weave them into the pattern. The first draft was necessary. Now turn the pages over and leave them upside down as you write the next draft.

Here are considerations for helping next drafts reveal the story's truth. These questions apply to prose pieces, but they'll guide revisions of poems, too.

1. Where should the story really begin?
2. Does every scene somehow advance the story?

3. Is the story overcrowded with people?

4. Is the story underpopulated?

5. Are important scenes played out in full detail?

6. Are minor events or scenes treated in too much detail?

7. Does all dialogue have a purpose—to advance the story, to reveal something about people and relationships?

8. Where should the story really end?

The next draft can add details to sharpen scenes, cut irrelevant details and insignificant scenes, and fill in missing pieces (for background and clarity). These drafts will take the story deeper.

True confessions: When I started my story "High Country," I wanted to write about my annual camping trips with some women friends and our dogs. On one trip, my strapping young Siberian husky jumped on my friend's small ancient dog and sent it rolling down a rocky hill. Recasting the people into fictional characters, I thought the story would be about Clemmie's guilt and her friend Leah's feeling of betrayal. I'd make the young dog actually cause the death of the old one, so it'd be even worse. But the first draft surprised me. The old dog wouldn't die, for one thing. More importantly, Leah started talking about her old mother who had Alzheimer's and Clemmie started thinking about her marriage. The story *was* about friendship, but not as I'd planned, and the other threads that decided to weave themselves in made for a much richer tapestry than I could have imagined.

The next draft eliminated the other women, the other dogs, and the other camping trips. It knocked away the first two pages and began closer to the real action. It cut some details and added some others. It revised the final scene to resolve the conflicts that had emerged in the first draft and to allow Clemmie a minor epiphany about her life.

Writer Ron Carlson had a few little suggestions, then, for the next draft. After the dog attack (yeah, it's still there), Clemmie and her dog escape the scene of the crime:

> "I'll leave you alone. I'll get my mutt out of here for a while." Clemmie and Bandit sidled away from camp and walked morosely out of the pines and around a pathless high meadow.
>
> When they returned, Leah had her tent down and her car loaded up.

Carlson's suggest was nothing more than "Add a beat here? Two sentences/description."

Here's the revised version:

> "I'll leave you alone. I'll get my mutt out of here for a while." Clemmie and Bandit sidled away from camp and walked morosely out of the pines and around a path- less high meadow. The high peaks were lit but the red and yellow groundcover was muted by shadow. The fog smoked away. At the lower curve was a stand of aspen, and Clemmie headed for the long naked trunks with their flares of yellow held high. Closer, though, she called the dog and turned around. The aspens had eyes scattered up the pale gray boles.
>
> When they returned, Leah was gone.

Adding those "beats" slowed things down a bit, let the reader see the scene and get a sense of Clemmie's feeling of guilt (even the trees, scary now, are watching her), and also speeded things up (eliminating the dragged-out, irrelevant details of Leah's departure and simply getting her gone).

I didn't think these things out, not until after I'd done them. Then I could look at the effects and decide whether or not they were true to Clemmie and her story.

The Big Questions

How can we tell if our stories are "true"? After I've let the process of writing at least three drafts do its work but before I begin the final touch-up stage, I ask myself nine sets of hard questions:

1. Is the story honest and true? Or have I held back out of some fear? Does the story matter to me?

2. Have I pushed it, really explored it, gone farther than I believed I could? Have I leapt into the sea rather than stayed on the comfortable, safe shore?

3. Is it real material, not just dinner-table chitchat? A charac- ter in J.R. Salamanca's novel *Southern Light* complains about another: "He used literature largely as a refuge from life, rather than as a fierce and passionate exploration of it." Is my material worthy of exploration?

4. Are my creations—no matter to what extent that they're based on real folks—living, breathing people on the page, not just cardboard cutouts? Do they act, rather than merely react? Does the narrator finally take charge and *do* something, rather than remain passive?

5. Have I told a story? Writer Rita Mae Brown said that "Art is moral passion married to entertainment. Moral passion without entertainment is propaganda, and entertainment without moral passion is television." Along with all my passion, have I also entertained along the way?

6. Does my story have a real plot rather than relying on coincidence or a string of events? Have I shown cause-and-effect relationships? Have I made connections?

7. Have I given attention to detail? Have I created the world of the story? Detail is the lifeblood of storytelling. Writer Shirley Jackson advised: "Always dress your ideas immediately." Have I let any abstract ideas run around naked in my story?

8. Does my story have a pattern? An order? James Baldwin wrote in "Autobiographical Notes": "One writes out of one thing only—one's own experience. Everything depends on how relentlessly one forces from this experience the last drop, sweet or bitter, it can possibly give. This is the only real concern of the artist, to recreate out of the disorder of life that order which is art." For years, that quote hung in 16-point type above my writing desk.

9. Have I been true to myself? When critics claimed that Samuel Barber's compositions had no style, he said it didn't matter. "I just go on doing, as they say, my thing. I believe this takes a certain amount of courage." Have I had the courage, finally, to make up my own mind, to trust myself?

Spray and Wash

It's difficult to be objective about our stories because we know how hard we've worked on them. A part of us wants to be recognized for all that labor, but the hard work mustn't show. So your last draft should involve careful line editing. The story in its final form will be so graceful and artful that it appears easy and artless. The writer has sweated, but the sweat stains can't mark the manuscript. Let's discuss some sweat stains to be laundered out.

Unnecessary Words

When "High Country" was accepted for publication, the editor asked (okay, demanded) that I cut it by three hundred words for a better fit in the magazine. Impossible! I thought. I'd revised the story thoroughly and every word was absolutely necessary. I wanted to see the story in print, so I went through it ruthlessly, excising filler words and nonessential phrases.

Here's the first paragraph with its cuts:

> Every fall, up from the desert, Clemmie and Leah camped another five hundred feet higher. The previous year they'd gotten drunk on margaritas at night and made an extravagant fire and cried about dogs dead or dying. Leah's Bud, an ancient terrier-something that smelled bad and looked, ~~Clemmie thought~~, like a burnt meatloaf, was the remains of a long-dead marriage to a press operator who had died ~~of cirrhosis~~ long after he'd left Leah and Budweiser. ~~The puppy had been a birthday present to him nineteen years ago.~~ Last fall, Leah had cried for the dying Bud—Clemmie remembered her coarse face, ocherous in the light of the fire, smoothed by tears—but here was Bud, still alive, on yet another final camping trip. Last year, Clemmie's own grief had been raw, with the white shepherd, who'd been her son's dog until he left for college, dead only two weeks. ~~After the dog had been buried~~, her son asked her to send some tufts of fur for memory's sake, and she'd finally found some ~~she hadn't vacuumed up~~ under the bed. This year Mark had again let her bring his dog, Bandit, a young husky ~~who was sweet at home but antisocial otherwise~~.

Thirty-four words gone and nothing really missed.

Perhaps every story needs an editor demanding 10 percent of the words be cut. Here are some words and phrases that are often easy to eliminate:

- *that* (He said ~~that~~ he wanted to go home.)
- *which* (The horse ~~which~~ he rode was black.)
- qualifiers such as *very* and *nearly* (The light was ~~sort of~~ dim.)
- wimpy words such as *appear* (~~It seemed that~~ he looked lonely.)

- *begin* and *start* (I ~~begin to~~ run up the trail.)

- *had* (In her memory, it ~~had~~ always rained on their camping trips, and the three of them ~~had~~ sat in the camper and ~~had~~ played Yahtzee.)

- phrases such as *he thought* and *she felt* (~~I felt that~~ nobody cared about me.)

- *there* and *it* at the beginning of sentences (~~There are~~ three witches crouched by the fire.)

- phrases that explain or state the obvious (~~In a fit of anger,~~ he punched his fist through the bathroom door.) ("Yeah, yeah, whatever," she said, ~~lost in thought.~~)

- many adjectives and most adverbs ("I love it here!" she said ~~happily~~, looking from the ~~spacious, open, sun-dappled~~ green clearing into the ~~infinitely dark, dense, primeval~~ jungle.)

Redundancies

Cut ~~unnecessarily repetitious and~~ redundant words and phrases. Here are a few samples culled from my reading:

- "Goddamnit!" Linda *cursed*.

- He stared at me *with his eyes*.

- His smile spread from ear to ear *upon his face*.

- I kicked at the dirt *with my feet*.

- She raised the apricot to her mouth and licked it *with her tongue*.

- My heart was beating fast *in my chest*.

- He thought *silently to himself*.

Oops

Sometimes what writers hear isn't quite what they mean when it's on the page. I am not making up these examples:

- He liked sleeping under the beautiful starlet skies.

- The windshield factor is in the minus forties.

- He's a real pain in the lower posterity.

- She ordered the bordello mushrooms.

- Todd launched a three point shot that went in as the buzzard sounded.

- She was homecoming queen and valid Victorian.

- And my favorite: We heard the cattle balling in the field.

The Unengaged Brain

Writers whose sprockets jumped their chains wrote these sentences:

- I've taken an interest in gymnastics ever since I was a sibling.

- He always held that special hole in his heart for Lily.

- Hemingway survived several fatal accidents.

- Gunfire and expositions filled the night.

- She was a brunette with large breasts wearing wire-rimmed glasses.

Mixed Metaphors

Metaphors that are mixed ought to be nixed. Examples:

- The new CEO ushered in the dawn of a new day. She tied up loose ends, hired new blood, and turned her attention to herding the rest of us cats. "I didn't want to touch the job with a ten-foot pole," she told me. "But it turned out to be a slam dunk."

- When traveling the Information Superhighway, remember that the grass is always greener when you can see the forest for the trees and that you'll be in hot water when the s**t hits the fan.

  Okay, I made those up. This wolf in sheep's clothing isn't the sharpest knife in the drawer, is she?

  Of course, such abominations don't always result from mixing clichés or expressions. Sometimes fresh metaphors confuse or cancel each other out. Examples:

- The ancient dog smelled bad and looked like a burnt meatloaf, a blackened brick in the rubble of a burned building . . .

- The aspens' long naked trunks with their flares of yellow held high rose from the meadow like ships' masts.

Clichés

As a kid, I knew better than to accept ABC gum. As a grown-up writer, I try to avoid Already-Been-Chewed words, too.

Here's a scene by my student Don Markham:

> "Don't let the cat out of the bag, and keep your ear to the ground," Sergeant Saturday says to the witness. "There is method to his madness. He will get his just desserts. Can you describe the suspect?"

> "He is larger than life, bright eyed and bushy tailed. At first blush, he is more than meets the eye," she says.

> "Just the facts, ma'am," says Sergeant Saturday. "Did he say anything?"

> "He said he was going to paint the town red, and pay the piper."

> "Anything else, ma'am?"

> "Without further ado, he rubbed me the wrong way. I told him he was up the creek with the wrong paddle. He read the handwriting on the wall, and beat a dead horse to death in one fell swoop."

> "Just the facts, ma'am, just the facts."

> "He said he was sick and tired of finding skeletons in his closet and taking the bull by the horns."

> "Anything else, ma'am?"

> "Once in a blue moon he drinks the milk of human kindness, and sows wild oats with a grain of salt."

> "Is that it, ma'am?"

> "One additional piece of information. He bit off more than he could chew, which is easier said than done. Then he faced the music, put his foot in his mouth and barked up the wrong tree."

> "Thank you, ma'am."

And thank you, Don. I think.

Writerisms

Certain words, phrases, and descriptions appear only on the page. Nobody actually utters lines such as these:

- He was ruggedly handsome and wore his hat at a rakish angle.

- She raised one classically shaped brow above her dancing eyes.

- A small smile played at the corners of her mouth.

- With that, he turned, rippling muscles shaking visibly.

Only in bad writing do brows knit, smiles tease corners of mouths, and flames lick (hungrily, of course). Only in writing are clothes donned, commands barked, sighs of relief breathed, reveries broken, and glances cast from beneath mops of thick hair. Only on the page do people chortle, chuckle, guffaw, quip, hiss, and muse.

Similarly, the use of "as," "while," and "-ing" phrases, especially attached to dialogue, happens on the artificial page, not in nature:

- "I tell you what," Tommy said as he discharged his pistol in the general vicinity of the target bottles, "one of these days that boy's gonna learn what it's like."

  The phrasing is inept, interrupting the dialogue as it does, and confusing (just how many shots is Tommy firing here while he speaks his fifteen words?).

  And because "as" and "while" mean that the action following them is happening at the same time as the action in the main part of the sentence, the construction leads to problems such as these:

- "Go get me another," Larry yells as he downs the last of his beer.

- "I'm glad you showed up," Ruth said while locking her lips on his.

  The simultaneous actions are impossible at worst, accidentally funny at best—poor Larry gurgling his line, poor Ruth ruining a no doubt perfectly good kiss with sucker-fish lips.

  Using the phrasing and stock descriptions they're used to seeing in print may, in the beginning, make writers feel professional. Then they learn to push aside the gauze of cliché and phony language, and to see clearly and describe honestly.

Body Parts

Keep 'em where they belong.

Here are actual lines from published stories, whose authors will remain mercifully anonymous:

- He tumbled into her eyes.

- His eyes slid down the front of her dress.

- She dragged her eyes away from his rugged-looking feet with an effort.
- His imagination ran rampant, ricocheting off the walls of his mind like a horsefly dazed by the heat.
- (He) felt his brain squirm in his skull.
- Emotion (is) the acid in my mind's stomach.
- Joint. Just thinking about Florence in that jarring bit of jargon always brought a mental smile to (his) Ph.D. trained ear.
- I want an explanation even when there really isn't one to be had. Not one I can reach out and feel swimming between the swollen bellies of my fingers, like motor oil.
- I felt a hollow pit in the base of my chest.
- His heart shot up, collided with the roof of his mouth.

Ouch.

Bad Images, Bad Metaphors

Reading pages aloud will expose atrocities such as these:

- His buttocks screamed in pain.
- Her eyes were still swollen from crying, swollen like jumbo shrimp.
- Nostalgia latched on like a Patriot missile.
- It was first light, and the sky offered a respite after emptying its bowels during the night.

And tongue twisters and puzzles such as these:

- ". . . huge water-walls rising only to suddenly fall onto frothy flatness, hot sun succeeding sleet succeeding harsh hail storms shrapnelling the sea succeeding snow succeeding sun."
- "He had breathed shallow gulps near golden-grassed gorges; but here today he lightly fumed in flurries of freedom in this city at the end of his rainbow."
- "Her shoulder muscles were aching with massive lactic acid."
- "The young mother cradled her baby with the dumb ambivalence of a frozen peach tree holding a Stern pot in its iced branches."

Down, boy. Bad metaphor, bad.

Turning Purple

Reading aloud and self-editing will identify minor stains, and then you can apply prewash and run them through the permanent press cycle. I confess to writing this line myself: "Anxiety filled her like a glutinous ball." The writers' group decided we ought to hold an annual fundraiser for starving writers—the Glutinous Ball.

But when the stains of sentimentality and overwriting penetrate too deeply, stories are incurably phony.

Intentional exaggeration may be the best way to teach ourselves to find the treatable spots and also to identify the indelible stains of dishonesty.

Here's a deliberately cheesy sample by my student Regina Heitzer-Momaday:

> "You are the apple of my eye," Myrna cooed adoringly.
>
> She looked at him lovingly with her eyes, at his soft white skin like milk and honey—whole and pure—at his eyes as big as saucers, at his eyelashes as soft as downy feathers, at his full and fresh mouth invitingly shaped like a heart. She herself didn't have the heart to tell him once and for all, to break the news to him with aplomb, that he was a foundling, that he was not her flesh and blood.
>
> She knew these certain facts: his father was a vampire, his mother was a zombie, and both his grandparents were werewolves. He didn't look at all like the amalgamous mixture he was.
>
> Or did he?
>
> He snarled audibly and started to lick her face with his long tongue.

Linda A. Ashburn, challenged to write the smarmiest scene possible, wrote this under the pseudonym Lucille J. Ashton (and who can blame her?):

> She silently screamed to herself as goosebumps spread over her like the skin of a pickle. Her heaving bosom heaved while she gazed about tentatively at the dark forms dancing around her. Her milky white thighs glowed from the stream of pale moonlight hitting them like milk from a

cow's udder. "Please don't hurt me!" she blurted as she gazed into their steely blue laughing eyes. The howling wind screamed through her partially opened window in the outside wall. Intensely hot flames licked her milky white thighs and heaving bosom and her sinewy flesh melted off of her thin strong bones and her blood coagulated as she writhed in agony. Her hair lit like the torch of the Statue of Liberty. Out of the rubble and ashes stepped one of the six young handsomely sexy broad-chested and brave firemen. He gazed at his partner and quipped, "She should've used smoke detectors."

Is it hot in here, or is it just me?

Practicing Purple

Your assignment is to write the most clichéd, smarmy, trite, cheesy piece of gooey screed possible. If you're stuck for a topic, try a love scene. This purple prose (purple poetry also allowed) should be no longer than one page.

I beg of you.

Why try "bad" writing, besides for laughs? First, exaggerating it will help you spot it when it accidentally creeps into the writing, in more benign form. Second, by understanding bad writing and its inherent phoniness, we understand good writing and the honesty that is its heart.

Knowing When to Quit

Some writers quit too soon. On the screen or printed out, drafts look like polished, published writing. It's tempting, it's easy, to save, post, send, submit.

And then, as with middle-of-the-night messages that are sent instead of saved as drafts for daylight scrutiny, the typos and the bad lines are exposed. More important, all the ways the story hasn't yet explored its depths are revealed.

Editors and contest managers can attest to the many submitters who ask to withdraw, revise, and resubmit their stories.

I hear writers excuse their rushed sloppiness: "This would be better if I'd had more time." We do have time, but we don't always spend enough of it on polishing, instead leaving the story in raw first or second draft stage, its potential unfulfilled. First creation is a rush, wild and charged. It's easy to become addicted to that rush, leaving each story as the earth was on the first day, "without form and void," with "darkness . . . upon the face of the deep," instead of going forward to shape raw creation, separating "the light from the darkness," the firmament from "the waters which were under the firmament . . . and the waters which were above the firmament," until the pages are the firmament and meaning runs deep beneath it and truth glows above it.

Some writers, though, don't know when to quit. Running a story by the writers' group with each tweaking is not the same as, alone at the desk, moving from draft to draft, taking the story all the way. H.G. Wells knew the truth about writers' groups and editors: "No passion in the world is equal to the passion to alter someone else's draft." It's impossible to answer everyone's "problem" with the story. Every correction or "improvement" inevitably results in yet another "problem." Endless polishing for the group's approval results in a story so shiny that it reflects nothing but the faces of those passionate rewriters and not your own special face.

Some writers keep on tinkering out of fear. It's scary to look upon the story and see that it is good and send it forth. But even God stopped on the seventh day rather than spend another week micromanaging.

And sometimes our creations frighten us. What are these beasts and creeping things we have brought to life? Maybe, we think, we'd better soften them and shrink them before they bite or sting someone. Wouldn't want to get sued. A mild and milky world is better for all, isn't it?

It's time to stop and take your hands off the story. You've created a world and ordered it. You could go on and pet it down into tameness and quiescence and it would disturb no one, including its creator. But readers and writers both sleepwalk through safe territory. In your risky world, readers are awake. Taking the risks of making that world has changed you and there's no retreating. Trust it. Leave the firmament jungly, the waters deep and swarming, the sky beating with thunder and lightning.

It is good.

I mean, it is true.

PERMISSIONS

ABOUT THE AUTHOR

MEG FILES is the author of *Meridian 144*, *The Third Law of Motion*, *Home Is the Hunter and Other Stories*, and *The Love Hunter and Other Poems*. She edited *Lasting: Poems on Aging*. Her poems, stories, and articles have appeared in anthologies and scores of magazines, including *Fiction*, *Mid-American Review*, *Iron Horse Literary Review*, *Writer's Forum*, *Oxford Magazine*, and *Crazyhorse*. She has taught creative writing at Colorado Mountain College, the University of Maryland, and Pima College where she directs the Pima Writers' Workshop. She has been a Bread Loaf fellow and the James Thurber Writer-in-Residence at Ohio State University.

INDEX

Books from Allworth Press

Allworth Press is an imprint of Skyhorse Publishing, Inc. Selected titles are listed below.

Author's Toolkit, Fourth Edition
by Mary Embree (5 ½ x 8 ½, 194 pages, paperback, $16.99)

Branding for Bloggers
by Zach Heller (5 ½ x 8 ½, 112 pages, paperback, $16.95)

Business and Legal Forms for Authors and Self-Publishers, Fourth Edition
by Tad Crawford, Stevie Fitzgerald, and Michael Gross
(8 ½ x 11, 176 pages, paperback, $24.99)

The Business of Writing: Professional Advice on Proposals, Publishers, Contracts, and More for the Aspiring Writer
Edited by Jennifer Lyons; foreword by Oscar Hijuelos
(6 x 9, 304 pages, paperback, $19.95)

The Fiction Writer's Guide to Dialogue
by John Hough, Jr. (6 x 9, 144 pages, paperback, $14.95)

Promote Your Book: Over 250 Proven, Low-Cost Tips and Techniques for the Enterprising Author
by Patricia Fry (6 x 9, 224 pages, paperback, $19.95)

Propose Your Book: How to Craft Persuasive Proposals for Nonfiction, Fiction, and Children's Books
by Patricia Fry (6 x 9, 288, paperback, $19.99)

Publish Your Book: Proven Strategies and Resources for the Enterprising Author
by Patricia Fry (6 x 9, 264, paperback, $19.95)

Starting Your Career as a Freelance Writer, Second Edition
by Moira Anderson Allen (6 x 9, 304 pages, paperback, $24.95)

Starting Your Career as a Freelance Editor
by Mary Embree (6 x 9, 240 pages, paperback, $19.95)

The Writer's Legal Guide, Fourth Edition
by Kay Murray and Tad Crawford (6 x 9, 352 pages, paperback, $19.95)

To see our complete catalog or to order online, please visit *www.allworth.com.*